In the Heart of the Earth

The Secret Code That Reveals What Is In the Heart of God

Ray Foucher

An in-depth and in-context examination of Matthew 12:40

"For as Jonas was three days and three nights in the whale's belly; so shall the Son of man be three days and three nights <u>in the heart of the earth.</u>"

authorHOUSE®

AuthorHouse™
1663 Liberty Drive
Bloomington, IN 47403
www.authorhouse.com
Phone: 1-800-839-8640

First published by AuthorHouse 6/12/2009

ISBN: 978-1-4389-6243-6 (e)
ISBN: 978-1-4389-6239-9 (sc)

Library of Congress Control Number: 2009902606

Printed in the United States of America
Bloomington, Indiana

This book is printed on acid-free paper.

Contents

Preface

Through careful investigation of this topic for a number of years I have received the blessings that come with in-depth study of God's word. I believe that anyone can follow a few simple principles of Bible study and that, if they carefully and prayerfully investigate, God will lead them to a deeper understanding of scripture. I am convinced that there are many more hidden truths in God's word and that He is steadily working to open our understanding and bring us back to the faith once delivered to our fathers in the earliest days of Christianity. If you share this belief, if you also think that there is more light to come from God's word, then you will enjoy and be stimulated by the thoughts presented in this book.

This study may challenge your understanding of some long-held Christian beliefs. However, if you will allow the Bible to be its own interpreter, if you will carefully follow the detailed logic, you will see that there is another way to understand the events around the resurrection of Jesus. Tradition, handed down for close to 2,000 years, has had its effect and, for many, the effect on their thinking is that it could not be any other way. Read with an open mind and pray that God will convict you of what is truth.

While I have looked at this topic from many different angles, I am sure there is much more that could be considered. For supplemental information, updates, submitting questions etc. go to this website: www.Jesus-resurrection.info.

Several appendices are separated from the main text in order to maintain its flow and ease of understanding. They are included to help answer the many questions that naturally come up when such different ideas are presented. Please read them as there is some very interesting material there.

Bible quotations are from the King James Version unless otherwise noted. Anything added in [square brackets] within Biblical quotations are my clarifications. Italicized words, as many editions of the King James Bible present them to indicate supplied words, are retained.

You will see that the implications of the conclusions are far-reaching. Some readers might even decide that important aspects of their Christian practice need to change. I pray that God will give you the strength to choose His way.

Ray Foucher

Introduction

God is love. This is the most important truth about God. Why then have so many become confused? God has been so misrepresented and misunderstood. He is no longer seen or appreciated as the God of love He really is. He can be understood to be a loving Father only as He is perceived as acting in a loving way toward others. This revelation has been given in the life of God's only-begotten Son. Jesus, while He walked among men, displayed a character of absolute, selfless love for others and He claimed:

"… he that hath seen me hath seen the Father …" (John 14:9)

Essentially, He said, "My character is just like my Father's" - like father, like son. What would a God of love be like? How would His character be manifest towards others in a way that we could see and understand? Early in our marriage, I gave my wife a plaque with the saying: "Let my love, like sunlight, surround you and yet give you illumined freedom." This comes close to expressing God's approach to us. In a loving relationship, love is not forced on another. There must be freedom to walk away from the relationship, or it is something other than love. God does not force anyone into a relationship with Him. He seeks to draw, to attract others to Him. He wants people to accept His ways so that He can bless His children now, and eventually with eternal life and "pleasures for evermore." (Psa 16:11)

> "If ye then, being evil, know how to give good gifts unto your children, how much more shall your Father which is in heaven give good things to them that ask him?" (Matt 7:11)

> "Thou hast given him his heart's desire, and hast not withholden the request of his lips. Selah." (Psa 21:2)

God does not force man to obey His laws. If He did, there would be no lying, stealing, murder, etc. If God arranged circumstances to keep these things from happening, He would necessarily be restricting man's free will. Obviously, He does not do this. He allows us the freedom to do what we want while, at the same time, seeking to illuminate our understanding that His way is the best for our happiness. He wants to give us "illumined freedom."

One of the greatest principles God uses in dealing with His people is to give them freedom of choice. Love can never be coerced. God only accepts love that is freely given to Him. More than that, God is completely devoted to doing the best He can for us.

> "Love … does not seek the things of itself …"
> (1 Cor 13:4-5, *KJ3 Literal Translation*)

Love seeks the good of others. Man makes it hard for God to bless him because he will not let go of sin. People want to follow their own wills instead of seeking to understand and follow God's will. How far will God go in allowing man to exercise his free will? Is there any ultimate demonstration of this in scripture? The answers lie in a passage of scripture that, at first glance, seems to have little to do with these questions.

It is a portion of scripture that has caused much confusion – Jesus' answer to the question of the scribes and Pharisees asking Him for a sign.

> "Then certain of the scribes and of the Pharisees answered, saying, Master, we would see a sign from thee. But he answered and said unto them, An evil and adulterous generation seeketh after a sign; and there shall no sign be given to it, but the sign of the prophet Jonas: For as Jonas was three days and three nights in the whale's belly; so shall the Son of man be three days and three nights in the heart of the earth." (Matt 12:38-40)

When He responded and said "there shall no sign be given to it, but …" He implied that, in answer to their request, one sign, and one sign only, would be given to them, to that generation, that "wicked and adulterous generation." There must have been something very significant about that sign.

Jesus mentioned aspects of Jonah's experience that related to His own experience of being "three days and three nights in the heart of the earth." Perhaps by closely examining the meaning of "three days and three nights," and "in the heart of the earth," and looking at the context of the whole passage, we will be better able to understand the meaning of the sign of Jonah and its relationship to our understanding of the character of God.

There are indications that some important original words in scripture have been translated incorrectly in many versions resulting in misunderstandings on important topics. This study will use the principle of letting the Bible interpret itself. This can be done by letting it define its own terms by examining how significant words are used in their contexts in other passages. That way, an interpretation is not being imposed; rather Biblical clues are uncovered to help discover the intended meaning.

More important than revealing and presenting a better Biblical understanding for some points of understanding about the resurrection, this study portrays God's character in a more complete way. For many readers, correctly understanding this passage of scripture will amount to the discovery of a secret code that reveals what is in the heart of God toward man. That you may be more impressed with the loveliness of His character, and have a deeper understanding of how He has dealt with His created beings, and how He seeks to relate to you is the object of this study.

Chapter 1 – The Context and the Method

Introduction

Context is always important when attempting to correctly understand scripture. Context includes both the immediate setting of the passage and the larger setting of the Bible as a whole with which it must be in harmony. Therefore it is necessary and very helpful when trying to understand particular words to examine how they are used elsewhere in scripture. This is the most significant method of analysis used in this book; that of letting the Bible define its own terms and interpret itself. Words change their meaning over time and our understanding of passages can easily be affected by our understanding of the word meanings. This method of study will be described later in this chapter.

To properly understand this important Bible passage in Matthew chapter 12 it is especially important to be familiar with the setting. This is described here in a narrative as it might have been written by one of Jesus' disciples whom I have named Jonah. The writing of Jonah's letter to a friend was set shortly after and concerning the events described in Matthew chapter 12. It follows, with some modifications, the text of Matthew. In Chapter Six, there is a second letter from Jonah in which he similarly relates the events of Matthew chapter 13, which further help to understand the passage. (Note that , in this letter by Jonah, pronouns referring to Jesus are not capitalized.)

The Setting, Jonah's First Letter

Greetings my dearest Julius,

If you remember, we met briefly here in Jerusalem and I promised to write to you. I'm sorry that probably three new moons have passed since then but much has happened in my life. We just had a Passover celebration here in Jerusalem, one of the saddest in my life – I'll tell you why.

You were curious about my name. I was named Jonah by my father as he had a special interest in the prophet Jonah, since both my father and I were born in Gathhepher, that prophet's birthplace. I feel kind of like that great prophet because, of course, he was called by God and ran the other way and, I fear, I am doing the same.

As we talked, you had expressed an interest in my association with the man Jesus of Nazareth but, of course, we didn't get time to talk much during our short visit. I want to write my story as best I can remember, both to share with you and to help myself better understand my own very-mixed feelings. Also, I am writing on this scroll because I have a desire to see a record of these remarkable events and I don't know that anyone else is recording them.

Everyone recalls the big stir that was caused by the one whom many say was a prophet who baptized in the wilderness. I was much saddened by news of his recent death at the command of King Herod. John had baptized many people and I was one of them. That was about two and a half years ago. The experience rekindled my faith in Yahweh and John's message got me thinking constantly about the promised Messiah that everyone seemed to be waiting for. Well, about a year ago now, I began hearing about another person that John had baptized. This was a man named Jesus, who was John's cousin, and the son of a now-deceased carpenter from Nazareth.

At that time, he had many followers who traveled occasionally with him to listen to him speak. I caught up with the group and joined them near the Lake of Galilee where Jesus was teaching. He also had a smaller, core group who spent almost all of their time with him.

Because of the often-unorthodox teachings of Jesus, the Pharisees were watching us most of the time. One advantage of the scrutiny of those fault finders was that they witnessed many miracles that Jesus performed. These were incredible, undeniable miracles, evidence of God's power and, in most cases, to heal the sick and the suffering. Of course, these miracles just brought Jesus into greater favor with the people, many of whom didn't have a very high regard for the Pharisees. I got the sense that, more than anything else, the Pharisees felt threatened by Jesus' growing popularity.

There is so much I could tell you, Julius, about this man and the things he taught but, rather than fill the many scrolls I could, I'll just relate the events of one day. It was an exceptional day to be sure, a sabbath and a day that I have been thinking about very much ever since. At that time Jesus went on the sabbath day through the grain fields; and we, his disciples, were hungry, so we began to pick heads of grain to eat. But when the Pharisees saw it, they said to him, "Behold, your disciples do that which is not lawful to do on the sabbath day." The first few times I was with the group when we did something like this on a sabbath I felt uneasy until I heard Jesus explain it to us. He would say things like, "The sabbath was made for man, and not man for the sabbath" and, as he talked on his favorite topic, the love of God, it made more sense to me. And so, we were just satisfying our hunger pangs when we fell again into the disfavor of the ever-watchful Pharisees. But he said to them "Haven't you read what David and those that were with him did, when they were hungry, how they entered the house of God, and ate the shewbread, which was not lawful for them to eat, but only for the priests? Or have you not read in the law, how that on the sabbath days the priests in the temple profane the sabbath, and are blameless?" I thought to myself: I knew Jesus would have an answer for them; good reasoning and, as always, from the word of God.

Then he continued, "But I say to you, that in this place is one greater than the temple." Oh, oh, I thought to myself. The Jews regard the temple as the most sacred object on earth. To claim anything or anyone was greater than the temple would not be appreciated by these Pharisees.

But Jesus had even more to say. "But if you had known what this means, I will have mercy, and not sacrifice, you would not have condemned the guiltless. For the Son of man is Lord even of the sabbath day." I liked the words he said about the guiltless because, in the eyes of those men, I was counted as guilty. Jesus, however saw nothing wrong with satisfying a real human need.

I have found, Julius, that as I have traveled with Jesus and watched him interact with the people they always felt as though he was their friend and even more that he would stand up for them against injustice. I learned that Jesus was far more concerned for the good of each person, no matter how low they were in society, than he was for the letter of the law. I should correct myself somewhat – he always obeyed God's law as originally given. It was the extra laws and minute specifications the Pharisees urged on the people, laws that seemed to make life worse, not better. Those were the ones Jesus disregarded.

The Pharisees didn't react directly to what Jesus said, they just whispered among themselves. Jesus paid them no more attention and when he was departed from there, he went into their synagogue. A number of us accompanied him and, as we found a place to sit, I saw some of the same Pharisees who, just a short while before, had accused us. We listened to the rabbis' teaching and took part in the service. Jesus could have given a far more interesting teaching than what we had to listen to but he was always careful not to unnecessarily offend others. We were just about to leave when some of the Pharisees, drawing attention to a man which had his hand withered, approached Jesus and asked him, "Is it lawful to heal on the sabbath days?" Once again, they were looking to accuse him. And he said to them, quite typically from what I had seen of his concern for anyone suffering, man or beast, "What man shall there be among you, that shall have one sheep, and if it fall into a pit on the sabbath day, will he not lay hold on it, and lift it out? How much is a man better than a sheep? Wherefore it is lawful to do well on the sabbath days." I thought to myself, if only these rigid Pharisees could understand, as I am beginning to, what God is really like.

There was a stirring among the Pharisees at Jesus' reply in anticipation of what he would do. Then he said to the man, "Stretch forth your hand." And he stretched it forth and it was restored whole like as the other. There was a great murmuring among everyone and then the Pharisees went out and, as I later learned, they held a council against him, how they might destroy him.

But when Jesus knew it, he withdrew himself from there and great multitudes followed him and he healed them all and charged them that they should not make him known. He wanted to avoid stirring up any more controversy than necessary. Indeed, he had not initiated the healing of the man with the withered hand but, when presented with the case by the Pharisees, his sympathy for the poor man just seemed to overwhelm him.

Jesus later explained his actions to us, again using the scriptures, saying it was "so that it might be fulfilled which was spoken by Isaiah the prophet, who said 'behold my servant, whom I have chosen; my beloved, in whom my soul is well pleased. I will put my spirit upon him and he shall shew judgment to the Gentiles. He shall not strive, nor cry; neither shall any man hear his voice in the streets. A bruised reed shall he not break and smoking flax shall he not quench till he send forth judgment unto victory. And in his name shall the Gentiles trust.'" I could see that this scripture was, in many ways, being fulfilled. The only problem I had was with the part about the Gentiles but I saw many things that indicated Jesus treated them quite differently than our religious leaders do.

While I was thinking this over, there was brought unto him one possessed with a devil, blind, and dumb and he healed him, insomuch that the blind and dumb both spake and saw. And all the people were amazed and said, "This cannot be the son of David can it?" They could not fathom that such a common looking man could be the promised Messiah. Personally, I was becoming more convinced that he might indeed be the much-looked-for Messiah.

Just as the people were saying this, our "friends" showed up again and when the Pharisees heard it, they said, "This fellow only casts out devils by Beelzebub the prince of the devils." As on other occasions, it seemed to me that Jesus knew their thoughts. He said to them, "Every kingdom divided against itself is brought to desolation and every city or house divided against itself shall not stand. And if Satan cast out Satan, he is divided against himself; how shall then his kingdom stand? And if I by Beelzebub cast out devils, by whom do your children cast them out? Therefore they shall be your judges. But if I cast out devils by the Spirit of God, then the kingdom of God is come unto you. Or else how can one enter into a strong man's house, and spoil his goods, except he first bind the strong man? And then he will spoil his house."

I thought to myself, "Sounds like another parable." Jesus often spoke in parables especially to the Pharisees and the people. At least he would usually explain what he said more plainly to us.

He continued, "He that is not with me is against me; and he that gathers not with me scatters abroad." "Sounds like a line drawn in the sand," I thought to myself. While Jesus did not go out of his way to antagonize these men, he would not back down when they accused him. He would stand his ground.

Jesus continued again "Wherefore I say unto you, all manner of sin and blasphemy shall be forgiven unto men but the blasphemy against the Holy Spirit shall not be forgiven unto men. And whoever speaks a word against the Son of man, it shall be forgiven him but whoever speaks against the Holy Spirit, it shall not be forgiven him, neither in this world, neither in the world to come."

I had to laugh to myself. The Pharisees were attributing deliverance from the demon – certainly a good thing, especially for the poor man himself – to the demons themselves. Jesus continued, pointing out the inconsistency of the Pharisees' reasoning and showing that if the results are good the cause must be good. He said "Either make the tree good, and his fruit good or else make the tree corrupt and his fruit corrupt for the tree is known by his fruit." Jesus was using the tree as a symbol of himself – a good tree producing good fruit. He went on to point out that the fruit of the Pharisees, especially as shown by their treatment of someone as unfortunate as this blind, dumb and demon-possessed man showed something about their characters. He spoke to them with pretty direct and seemingly-harsh words but, as always, his tone of voice was not condemning but full of love and concern for even these unjust men. He said to them "How can you, offspring of vipers, being evil, speak good things? For it is out of the abundance of the heart that the mouth speaks. A good man out of the good treasure of the heart speaks good things and an evil man out of the evil treasure speaks evil things. But I say to you, that every idle word that men speak, they shall give account for in the day of judgment. For by your words you will be justified and by your words you will be condemned."

Jesus was getting to something more important now. The Pharisees were always questioning Jesus' actions and words. But, of course, it was really more his character that they were targeting. While he would make references to his Father - and they knew he was not talking about Joseph the carpenter - they would try to associate him with anything else, in this case, even directly with the demons. Now he was calling into question their lineage, referring to them as offspring of vipers, not simply in a physical sense but more in terms of character. Of course, they would always claim Abraham as their Father and even John the Baptist had chided them for doing that. Jesus kept pointing to and talking of the heavenly Father, clearly claiming him as his Father. The more I saw and heard it the more I began to hope that the Father is like what I am seeing in the life of Jesus. These claims and counter claims just seemed to go back and forth without resolution but with the effect that the people seemed to take Jesus' side more of the time. It was almost, it seemed to me, from a sense of desperation that certain of the scribes and of the Pharisees answered saying "Master, we would see a sign from thee."

I knew what they wanted. It wasn't so much just a miracle – they had seen many miracles. I sensed that they were demanding something that would clearly show his relationship to the Father. He kept talking of the Father in ways they couldn't relate to. Their sense of the Father was that of a severe, exacting judge. If Jesus was from the Father in heaven, they wanted a miracle as proof. I think it would have taken something like fire from heaven to burn up the hated Romans, to satisfy them.

They asked Jesus for a sign but he answered and said to them, "An evil and adulterous generation seeks after a sign and there shall no sign be given to it but the sign of the prophet Jonah. For as Jonah was three days and three nights in the whale's belly; so shall the Son of man be three days and three nights in the heart of the earth."

This caught my attention even more as I heard the name of Jonah. I knew very well the story of Jonah and the whale. It also got me wondering what he was referring to. It wasn't until I connected some of the things he said later that day that I even began to understand what he meant.

Jesus went on in his reply, "The men of Nineveh shall rise in judgment with this generation and shall condemn it: because they repented at the preaching of Jonas and, behold, a greater than Jonas is here. The queen of the south shall rise up in the judgment with this generation and shall condemn it: for she came from the uttermost parts of the earth to hear the wisdom of Solomon and, behold, a greater than Solomon is here." He seemed to be saying that, while the people of pagan Ninevah repented at the preaching of the prophet Jonah, the Pharisees would not repent even though someone greater than Jonah was present, referring to himself. Then he seemed to elevate himself above even wise Solomon. I knew that Jesus had incredible wisdom but this claim would not sit well with these Pharisees.

Then he continued and his words sounded even more like a parable. "When the unclean spirit is gone out of a man, he walks through dry places seeking rest and finds none. Then he says, I will return into my house from where I came out and when he is come, he finds it empty, swept and garnished. Then he goes and takes with himself seven other spirits more wicked than himself and they enter in and dwell there and the last state of that man is worse than the first. Even so shall it be also to this wicked generation."

While he yet talked to the people, I saw his mother and his brethren standing without, desiring to speak with him. So, when I got a chance, I said to Jesus, "Behold, your mother and your brethren are standing outside and want to speak with you." He answered and said to me (and perhaps also for the benefit of others around), "Who is my mother and who are my brethren?" And he stretched out his hand toward his disciples, and said, "Behold my mother and my brethren. For whoever shall do the will of my Father which is in heaven, the same is my brother, and sister, and mother." The sweep of his arm seemed to include me, which I appreciated.

Julius, I would like to tell you about the rest of the events of that day. We all – Jesus, us disciples and the whole multitude - went down to the sea side where he taught many things. I would love to tell you, but I will have to do that another time. I must close this letter for now but will, regretfully, end it on a sad note.

There were many things Jesus said that I had some difficulty with and I became somewhat less enthusiastic about following him. They just did not fit with my understanding of the role of the promised Messiah, Israel's deliverer. A few months later, Jesus was teaching in the synagogue in Capernaum and said some things that many of his disciples had a hard time accepting. From that time many of his disciples went back, and walked no more with him. With very mixed feelings, I also am no longer traveling with him. I do know in my heart that this man is at least sent from God and perhaps much more.

I still don't completely understand what he said about the sign of Jonah. He said that he, the son of man, as he often referred to himself, would be three days and three nights in the heart of the earth. It seemed to me, knowing that Jesus spoke so much in parables and from what he taught later that day, that he was talking about himself somehow being within the control of man for a period of time. He has certainly been on, or in, my heart and in my thoughts during the last few months. But I cannot conceive of our promised Messiah doing anything other than rising to his rightful position as the leader and liberator of Israel.

I just know, from the way he said it and the circumstances at the time, that there is something very significant about the sign he referred to. I will have to wait and hopefully it will become clear.

Until next time, Julius, may Yahweh's blessings be upon you.

Your friend, Jonah.

The Method

Because word meanings can change over time, there are certain words for which determining the meaning from the way the Bible uses them instead of from a dictionary, a concordance or our own understanding, can help arrive at the correct meaning.

"Knowing this first, that no prophecy of the scripture is of any private interpretation."
(2 Pet 1:20)

"Private interpretation" would include interpretations by the authors of dictionaries or concordances, or anyone using those tools. The other way to interpret is to examine how the Bible itself uses the words under investigation.

> We need to let the Bible itself tell us what difficult words and phrases mean. Surely, it is an authority on its own meaning.

One of the clearest examples in this study is regarding the use of the word "heart" which is translated from the Greek work "kardia" and used in the phrase "in the heart of the earth." We'll find in Chapter Two that it is consistently used with the sense of man's mind, his thinking and emotions. This has the potential to change our understanding of the phrase "in the heart of the earth" where "heart" has traditionally been understood to mean the center, or middle.

Another related method that will help in this investigation is to understand that scripture is consistent and without contradiction - after all, God is the author. In scripture, Jesus made a number of statements like:

"… he that hath seen me hath seen the Father …" (John 14:9)

Since He also said, "No man hath seen God at any time …" (John 1:18) we can understand that He meant that while no man has physically seen the Father with his eyes, those that have seen or perceived Jesus' character have essentially seen, and will understand the Father's character, as they are the same.

If Jesus and His heavenly Father have the same characters, we can expect that they would act the same in similar circumstances. This will help us understand the deepest layers of meaning of this scripture referring to "the sign of the prophet Jonas," and to Jesus being "in the heart of the earth."

In the New Testament, we read of Jesus saying:

"But I say unto you which hear, <u>Love your enemies</u>, do good to them which hate you," (Luke 6:27)

"But I say unto you, That ye resist not evil: but whosoever shall smite thee on thy right cheek, turn to him the other also." (Matt 5:39)

We never read in the gospels of Jesus harming anyone. He went about only doing good and helping in every circumstance. Then we read examples of God bringing destruction upon His enemies and, eventually, consigning them, it seems to say, to burn forever:

> "Then shall he say also unto them on the left hand, Depart from me, ye cursed, into <u>everlasting fire</u>, prepared for the devil and his angels:" (Matt 25:41)

> And these shall go away into <u>everlasting punishment</u>: but the righteous into life eternal." (Matt 25:46)

> "And the devil that deceived them was cast into the lake of fire and brimstone, where the beast and the false prophet *are* and shall be tormented day and night <u>for ever and ever</u>. And whosoever was not found written in the book of life was cast into the lake of fire." (Rev 20:10, 15)

Burning someone forever for a mere lifetime of sin certainly does not seem like justice. Clearly, there is an apparent difference in character between the two groups of verses above.

What people tend to do with such discrepancies is to choose one viewpoint or the other, and collect those verses that support their viewpoint and disregard the rest. However, the proper way to approach understanding the Bible is to recognize that there is internal consistency in the Word and that God Himself is consistent and, in fact, unchanging:

> "For I am the LORD, I change not ..." (Mal 3:6)

Of course, we tend to use our understanding of words to understand scripture. We should keep in mind that God says:

> "For My thoughts are not your thoughts, neither are your ways My ways, saith the Lord. For as the heavens are higher than the earth, so are My ways higher than your ways, and My thoughts than your thoughts." (Isa 55:8-9)

Perhaps we need to consider that our definitions of words cannot always be used to understand God's ways. Also, as described above, the Bible simply uses some words differently than we have come to understand them. This will resolve many difficulties and apparent contradictions.

In the example of the punishment of the wicked, perhaps resolution can be found by examining how the Bible itself uses words such as "eternal," "everlasting" and "forever and ever." In the Old Testament, the words "everlasting" and "for ever" sometimes signify a very limited time.

Here is an example of eternal fire:

> "Even as Sodom and Gomorrha ... are set forth for an example, suffering the vengeance of <u>eternal fire</u>." (Jude 1:7)

This shows that eternal fire can be something that does eventually go out, in this case:

> " ... turning the cities of Sodom and Gomorrha into ashes ..." (2 Pet 2:6)

Let's look at some further examples. Because his servant, Gehazi, practiced deceit, Elisha declared:

> "The leprosy therefore of Naaman shall cleave unto thee, and unto thy seed <u>for ever</u>. And he went out from his presence a leper *as white* as snow."
> (2 Kings 5:27)

We don't understand from this that Gehazi's family would never end, and their leprosy would never end.

The servant of an Israelite who decided to stay with his master even when he was free to leave was to be treated, as God directed, in a certain way:

> "Then his master shall bring him [the servant] unto the judges; he shall also bring him to the door, or unto the door post; and his master shall bore his ear through with an aul; and he shall serve him <u>for ever</u>." (Exo 21:6)

How could a servant serve his master for ever? Will there be servitude in the world to come?

Jonah, describing his time in the whale, said:

> "I went down to the bottoms of the mountains; the earth with her bars *was* about me <u>for ever</u>: yet hast thou brought up my life from corruption, O LORD my God." (Jonah 2:6)

Yet we are told that:

> " … Jonah was in the belly of the fish <u>three days and three nights</u>."
> (Jonah 1:17)

Really, this is a rather short "for ever." Understanding "for ever and ever," "eternal" and "everlasting" as the Bible defines them resolves the apparent contradiction pointed out above. This also brings consistency with verses such as:

> "For, behold, the day cometh, that shall burn as an oven; and all the proud, yea, and all that do wickedly, shall be stubble: and the day that cometh shall burn them up, saith the Lord of hosts, that <u>it shall leave them neither root nor branch</u>."
> (Mal 4:1)

It should now be clear that when the words "for ever and ever" are interpreted according to dictionary definitions, a certain understanding will emerge, while if the Bible's own usage of the words is used to determine its meaning, then a very different understanding becomes clear. The nature of "forever" in a particular use is understood to be related to the nature of situation. For mortal man it may be as long as life lasts. For God who is immortal it can indeed mean without end.

For some problem words, the only safety is in discarding dictionary definitions and using the Bible as its own dictionary and, therefore, as its own interpreter. Done properly this method will remove contradictions and haramonize all the scriptures on a topic with no need to disregard seemingly-contradictory statements.

Whenever a word causes a serious problem or contradiction as understood in the common way, it should be examined carefully and its meaning determined from its scriptural context. In this study, effort has been made to do this for a number of significant words.

Chapter 2 – Three Days and Three Nights

"Then certain of the scribes and of the Pharisees answered, saying, Master, we would see a sign from thee. But he answered and said unto them, An evil and adulterous generation seeketh after a sign; and there shall no sign be given to it, but the sign of the prophet Jonas: For as Jonas was three days and three nights in the whale's belly; so shall the Son of man be three days and three nights in the heart of the earth." (Matt 12:38-40)

This passage of scripture has caused considerable controversy. Many people recognize a problem with the reference to three days and three nights. This has resulted in such things as the popular Wednesday crucifixion theory which will be discussed in Chapter Four. Others see the crucifixion as happening on Thursday. The arguments against Christianity and the written word coming from the confusion over this passage often go something like the following:

"Christianity depends on the 'death' of Jesus for salvation. Jesus claimed that while 'in the heart of the earth' He would be as Jonah was while 'in the whale's belly.' The contradiction between His words and the fulfillment is obvious. Jonah was alive, Jesus was dead! Jesus had said 'like Jonah' not 'unlike Jonah.' Thus, according to His own test, Jesus was not the true Messiah of the Jews.

Also, the prophesied time was not fulfilled. No matter how hard you try, you cannot get three days <u>and</u> three nights out of a Friday afternoon death and a Sunday morning resurrection. If Jesus' own prophecy doesn't stand, how can anything else in scripture?" (Adapted from various comments on the internet.)

Honest Christians have to admit that this passage does not seem to be as clear as it might. They often don't know how to present the truth to clear up the situation. They present arguments that are not convincing to those who hold critical positions as described above. People who argue against the Biblical record are assuming that Jesus meant He would be in the tomb for three days and three nights as Christians commonly understand that time period and that, since He was to be like Jonah, He would also have to be alive. This chapter will carefully examine the phrase "three days and three nights" to Biblically determine the real beginning and end of that period and Jesus' whereabouts and condition during this time. It will solve the arguments raised above and more, and raise other questions that will be dealt with in further chapters.

Try as hard as you want, you cannot get three days and three nights out of
a Friday afternoon crucifixion and a Sunday morning resurrection.

Jonah and the Whale

To correctly understand Jesus' experience it is necessary to first examine Jonah's. How long did Jonah spend in the whale? Scripture says "three days and three nights."

> "Now the LORD had prepared a great fish to swallow up Jonah. And Jonah was in the belly of the fish three days and three nights." (Jonah 1:17)

How long is that? It might look like this:

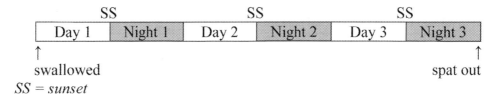

Of course, the days and nights could be switched in their order because it does not say at what hour Jonah was swallowed. However, the verse does number the days first. The more important question is, "does it have to be exactly or something very close to 72 hours?"

Inclusive Reckoning

Many Bible students will bring up the Middle Eastern concept of inclusive reckoning. People of the Middle East and other cultures did, and still do this, with the ages of their children. As soon as they are born they are considered to be one year old. Western culture would think of them as being in their first year, but they call it one year old. Then, when they pass the New Year, they are referred to as two years old – they are in their second year (relative to the cycle of years). If a child is born one day before the start of the New Year, he is one year old. The next day, when the New Year has begun, he would be referred to as two years old (he is in his second year going by the calendar year). Westerners would say he is still less than one year old, relative to the anniversary of his birth. Inclusive reckoning counts any part of a year as a whole year and does the same with shorter time periods.

Since any part of a day can be counted as a whole day and since evening and morning (See *Appendix 1 - Variations in Use of the Word "Even" as in Evening*, p. 120), Biblically, constitute one day ("… the evening and the morning were the first day." Gen 1:5) a three-day time period could be as short as:

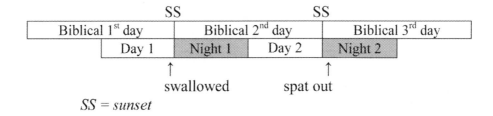

Let's count the days:

> The **first** day is a short portion of day one from when Jonah was swallowed until sunset.
> The **second** day it the next whole evening and morning (labeled as "night 1" and "day 2") from sunset to sunset.
> The **third** day is a short portion of the next night (labeled as "night 2") from sunset until Jonah was spat out.

This would count as three days according to Jewish inclusive reckoning but in the western system it is really one complete 24-hour day plus a short time on the preceding day, and another short time on the following day, perhaps 26 hours.

> If you lived in many parts of the Middle East, you would be
> considered to be one year old on the day you were born.

But Jesus Said …

While this is legitimate when counting a specified number of days, in this case, the time designated by Jesus was a number of days <u>and</u> a number of nights. It was not just a number of days where a portion of a day could count as a whole day. But it was three days <u>and</u> three nights. To satisfy the designated time, Jonah must have been in the belly of the whale for three days, or portions thereof, and three nights or portions thereof – something much closer to 72 hours.

In reference to His time in the heart of the earth, Jesus clearly said "three days <u>and</u> three nights." Notice, He said it twice in this one passage:

> "… and there shall no sign be given to it, but the sign of the prophet Jonas: For as Jonas was <u>three days **and** three nights</u> in the whale's belly; so shall the Son of man be <u>three days **and** three nights</u> in the heart of the earth." (Matt 12:39-40)

According to the usual understanding of Jesus' time in the tomb, how close can we come to the specification of "three days <u>and</u> three nights"? Most Christians believe that Jesus was crucified and died on Friday afternoon, was buried shortly before sundown Friday, rested in the tomb over the Sabbath (Friday sunset to Saturday sunset) and was resurrected early on Sunday morning. Let's check that in scripture:

> "This *man* [Joseph of Arimathaea] went unto Pilate, and begged the body of Jesus. And he took it down, and wrapped it in linen, and laid it in a sepulchre that was hewn in stone, wherein never man before was laid. And that day was the preparation, [Friday] and the sabbath [starting at Friday sunset] drew on. And the women also, which came with him from Galilee, followed after, and beheld the sepulchre, and how his body was laid. And they returned, and prepared spices and ointments; and rested the sabbath day [Friday sunset – Saturday sunset] according to the commandment." (Luke 23:52-56)

The next verse speaks of "the first day of the week, very early in the morning …" (Luke 24:1) but John is even a little more specific indicating that Mary arrived before sunrise:

> "The first *day* of the week [Saturday sunset to Sunday sunset] cometh Mary Magdalene early, when it was <u>yet dark</u>, [before sunrise Sunday morning] unto the sepulchre, and seeth the stone taken away from the sepulchre." (John 20:1)

So, how many days and nights was Jesus in the tomb? Let's diagram it according to the usual understanding of the scriptures quoted above:

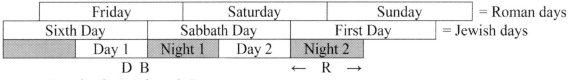

D = death; B = burial; R = resurrection

How long was Jesus in the tomb?

> **Day one** was from Friday late afternoon from His burial, to sunset – probably less than an hour, but we'll use inclusive reckoning and count it as one day.
> **Night one** was from Friday sunset, the start of Sabbath, to Saturday morning at sunrise – one full night.
> **Day two** was from Saturday sunrise to Saturday sunset, the light part of the Sabbath – one full day.
> **Night two** was from Saturday sunset, until sometime before sunrise Sunday morning - a few minutes to almost 12 hrs. We know that He rose before sunrise, but, at this point in the study, not how long before. Again, we'll use inclusive reckoning and count it as one full night.

So, we have for the number of days:

> About an hour late Friday afternoon   = 1 day (using inclusive reckoning)
> All of the light part of Saturday   <u>= 1 day</u>
>   Total = 2 days

And we have, for the number of nights:

Friday evening sunset to Saturday morning sunrise   = 1 night

Saturday evening sunset to the resurrection

    sometime before sunrise on Sunday morning   <u>= 1 night</u>

                                 Total = 2 nights

How can one get three days and three nights out of this? – It's not possible even by using inclusive reckoning. Of course, most people will just consider the days, or portions of days, and use inclusive reckoning to come up with three days. However, that is not what Jesus said. Again, He said:

> "For as Jonas was three days and three nights in the whale's belly; so shall the Son of man be three days and three nights in the heart of the earth." (Matt 12:40)

"Three days <u>and</u> three nights." The count of the number of days and nights from the diagram above results in, at most, two days and two nights.

Is "a Day and a Night" Equivalent to "a Day"?

Some people would argue that the time periods "three days and three nights," "after three days" and "three days" are simply all equivalent, because they are used interchangeably to refer to the same event. Obviously, a time period referred to as "a day and a night" could be the equivalent of "a day," where "a day" could be less than a full 24-hour day.

However, "a day" reckoned inclusively may or may not be equivalent to "a day and a night." If the "day" included only an hour or two during daylight hours, then it is not equivalent to "a day <u>and</u> a night" because there is no night, or portion of a night.

Used inclusively, the more general term "day" allows for a time span of anywhere from a moment in a day, whether during the dark or light portion, to a full 24 hours from sunset to sunset.

The more-specific term "a day and a night," also used inclusively, could refer to as short a time as from a just moment before sunset to just a moment after sunset and including some of the day and some of the night:

SS = sunset; S = start of day and night; E = end of day and night

Or "a day and a night" could refer to as long a time period as up to almost a full twelve hours before sunset, and up to almost a full twelve hours after sunset:

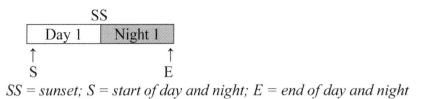

SS = sunset; S = start of day and night; E = end of day and night

Either of the above or anything in between, used inclusively, could qualify as "a day and a night." The point to be understood is that a day and a night must include some of each. Therefore, three days and three nights must include at least parts of three consecutive days (light portions) and it must include at least parts of three consecutive nights (dark portions).

Compare the following verse:

> "Thrice was I beaten with rods, once was I stoned, thrice I suffered shipwreck, a night and a day I have been in the deep." (2 Cor 11:25)

For Paul to be able to say that he spent "a night <u>and</u> a day in the deep," he must have spent at least some portion of a day, and some portion of a night in the deep. A few hours treading water in the middle of the day, even used inclusively, would not match what he said.

From what Jesus actually said, from the evidence of Paul's experience and some logical reasoning we can see that the time period Jesus specified would best be fulfilled by something more than the usual Friday afternoon to Sunday morning scenario. We can also see why there would be confusion and skepticism over the common understanding.

In the Heart of the Earth

Here is an apparent problem: Clearly, Jesus was not in the tomb for three days and three nights. We take it for granted that He, who said He was "the Truth," always told the truth, therefore His words need to be examined more carefully. Did He say He would be "in the tomb" for three days and three nights? No. So what did He actually say? He said that He would be "<u>in the heart of the earth</u>." An obvious possibility is that the "tomb" and the "heart of the earth" are not the same; that they are in fact, different places.

> Did Jesus even say He would be in the tomb? No, He said
> He would be "in the heart of the earth." But where is that?

Different places! It has always been assumed that "in the heart of the earth" refers to the grave but is that really what it means? Please recognize that to say that "the heart of the earth" represents the grave, is an assumption. Remember that Jesus often spoke in parables in which the meaning was hidden just below the surface or apparent meaning of the words used. Also, Jesus could have simply given the time and the place without adding the reference to Jonah. He didn't have to link His future experience to Jonah's previous experience. Why did He do it? There must be something significant about Jonah's experience that relates to Jesus' experience.

Jesus and Jonah Compared

Let's compare Jesus' experience more closely to that of Jonah. We need to find a clue in the experience of Jonah that will help us understand Jesus' experience. The thing to do is to look more closely at what the two experiences had in common.

	Time-common	Place-not common
Jonah was	3 days and 3 nights	in the whale's belly
Jesus was	3 days and 3 nights	in the heart of the earth

They both spent three days and three nights in their respective places or conditions – the time factor was common to both of them. However, one was in the belly of the whale, the other was in the heart of the earth – the location was not common. That's time and location, but how about the premise: "as" one was, "so" shall be the other? The scripture said:

> "… as Jonas was three days and three nights in the whale's belly; so shall the Son of man be …" (Matt 12:40)

The wording suggests that something about their condition was similar. The emphasis was not on as long as Jonah was, so long shall Jesus be. The time was the same, but time was not the emphasis. Also, the emphasis was not where Jonah was, there shall Jesus be. The location was not the most important part. (Indeed, the locations were different.) The emphasis was as Jonah was, so shall Jesus be – the emphasis was on their respective conditions.

> Jesus was compared to Jonah not primarily in terms of time or of location, but rather, in terms of condition.

The words "as" and "be" speak of condition or state of being. Let's look for something else they might have had in common that fits not the place or the length of time, but rather their condition. When Jonah was in the belly of the whale he was alive. When Jesus was in the tomb He was dead – so they didn't have that in common. It is interesting that we have always understood that Jesus was dead for three days and three nights. We read "as Jonas was … so shall the Son of man be …" and compare His experience, His condition, to that of Jonah, yet Jonah was not dead!

It doesn't work. The scripture reads, "as Jonah was … so shall the son of man be …" There must have been something similar regarding their respective conditions. What else was there about the condition of Jonah that might have been similar to Jesus' experience? Here are some verses David wrote about his own experience that seem to be related:

"The sorrows of death compassed me, and the floods of ungodly men made me afraid. The sorrows of hell <u>compassed me about</u>: the snares of death prevented me." (Psa 18:4-5)

"I am counted with them that go down <u>into the pit</u>: I am as a man *that hath* no strength: ... Thou hast laid me in the lowest pit, in darkness, in the deeps." (Psa 88:4, 6)

While not speaking of Jesus, these verses relate death, or fear of death, to thoughts of being surrounded, of being in water, of being threatened by ungodly men, of being confined. Here is a verse where Jonah is describing his experience:

"I went down to the bottoms of the mountains; <u>the earth with her bars *was*</u> about me for ever: yet hast thou brought up my life from corruption, O LORD my God." (Jonah 2:6)

What is suggested by being "compassed about," "snares" and "bars"? How about imprisonment, confinement, no escape? What was common in the condition of Jesus and Jonah? It was definitely not that they were both dead. Could it be that they somehow were both confined in a place, or by circumstances, for the same length of time?

	Time-common	**Place-not common**	**Condition-common**
Jonah was	3 days and 3 nights	in the whale's belly	confined
Jesus was	3 days and 3 nights	in the heart of the earth	confined

They were both confined: Jonah in the whale and Jesus, even if it was only figuratively, in the heart of the earth. Remember, we are just exploring possibilities at this point. Now, we need to look more carefully at where and in what manner Jesus might have been, in a sense, confined. Where was He during the three days and three nights? We've already seen that there is a problem with the idea that He was in the tomb for three days and three nights, because He wasn't. So the question comes down to: where, or what, is the heart of the earth? Most people, of course, cannot consider that it is anything other than the grave. However, we need to "think outside the box." Specifically, we need to let scripture define its own terms. How does the Bible explain what Jesus meant when He said He would be "three days and three nights in the heart of the earth?" Let's first establish more firmly, from scripture, that He was not talking about being in the grave for that length of time.

Where Was Jesus for the Three Days and Three Nights?

Jesus did say He would be "three days and three nights in the heart of the earth." However, He did not use the word tomb or grave. The word "grave" was in Jesus' vocabulary and there is record of Him using it on at least two occasions:

> "Woe unto you, scribes and Pharisees, hypocrites! For ye are as <u>graves</u> which are not seen, and the men that walk over *them* are not aware *of them*." (Luke 11:44)

> "Marvel not at this: for the hour is coming, in the which all that are in the <u>graves</u> shall hear His voice." (John 5:28)

In both cases, the word "graves" is translated from the Greek word "mnemeion" (*Strong's* NT#3419). The King James Version translates "mnemeion" as "sepulchre" 29 times, as "grave" 8 times, and as "tomb" 5 times.

If Jesus had meant what most people think He meant, the gospels could have just recorded Him as saying, "As Jonas was three days and three nights in the whale's belly; so shall the Son of man be three days and three nights in the grave," with the Greek text using the word "mnemeion."

> Why did Jesus say He would be "in the heart of the earth"?
> The earth doesn't have a heart.

However, this word was not used. Instead, He used the rather strange phrase "in the heart of the earth." Let's examine this phrase carefully. Does it have a meaning beyond its most obvious and beyond what everyone thinks or has assumed it means?

A Word Study of "Heart"

The Greek word translated in this verse as "heart" is "kardia" (*Strong's* NT#2588), which is similar to the English terms "cardia" or "cardiac." The King James Version translates it consistently; 159 times as "heart" and once as "broken hearted." Here are the major meanings provided by the *Online Bible Greek Lexicon*:

1. That organ in the animal body which is the centre of the circulation of the blood, and hence was regarded as the seat of physical life.
2. Denotes the centre of all physical and spiritual life.
3. Of the middle or central or inmost part of anything, even though inanimate.

In modern English, "heart" is also used to mean the center of something, but did Bible writers have that understanding, and more specifically, did they ever use the word "kardia" with that meaning?

An examination, including the context, of all 160 uses of the Greek word "kardia" in the New Testament will show that there is not another verse where it has been used in the sense of the "middle" or "center" of anything.

The only meaning listed among the Greek Lexicon definitions for kardia that might relate to being in the earth is the last one, and it specifies "the middle or central or inmost part." If the phrase "in the heart of the earth" (Matt 12:40) is understood to be referring to the heart of the physical earth - it doesn't work because Jesus, while in the grave, wasn't anywhere near "the middle, or central, or inmost part" of the earth, which was a few thousand kilometers away. Rather, He was near the surface of the earth, in a cave, probably laid on a slab of stone prepared for that purpose, wrapped in burial clothes and not even directly covered by any earth or dirt.

We understand "in the heart of the earth" to mean in the middle of, or at least somewhere in the earth, for two reasons. One is because that is one way we use the word "heart." The second reason is because of tradition that has been passed down to us. However, there is no justification for the common understanding that "in the heart of the earth" means in the grave. This is a good case of letting the Bible define its own terms through examining the context, to see how the Bible itself uses words.

> We understand that "heart" can mean the physical middle of something, but when did that meaning come into use in the English language?

There actually is another Greek word, "mesos," (*Strong's* NT#3319) that could have been used to refer to being "in the center of the earth" if that was the intent of the phrase. Its definitions as given by the *Online Bible Greek Lexicon* are:

1) middle
2) the midst
3) in the midst of, amongst

Here are some examples where the Greek word "mesos" is translated as "midst" in the King James Version:

> "But the ship was now in the <u>midst</u> of the sea, tossed with waves: for the wind was contrary." (Matt 14:24)

> "Where they crucified him, and two other with him, on either side one, and Jesus in the <u>midst</u>." (John 19:18)

> "Then Paul stood in the <u>midst</u> of Mars' hill, and said, *Ye* men of Athens, I perceive that in all things ye are too superstitious." (Acts 17:22)

This would have been the word to use in a phrase referring to being buried in the midst of some location. For more on the Biblical use of "kardia" see *Appendix 2 – Cases of "Kardia" Translated "Heart" as Understood in this Study*, p. 121.

A Word Study of "Earth"

Let's now consider the other important word in the phrase, "in the heart of the earth." The word "earth" used here is translated from the Greek word "ge" (*Strong's* NT#1093) for which the possible meanings given in *Strong's Concordance* are:

> "soil; by extension a region, or the solid part or the whole of the terrene globe <u>(including the occupants in each application)</u>:-country, earth (-ly), ground, land, world."

This is reasonable, that the same word could mean either the earth or its occupants. Remember, as the following verses say, that we are made from the dust of the earth:

> "In the sweat of thy face shalt thou eat bread, till thou return unto the ground; for out of it wast thou taken: for dust thou *art*, and unto dust shalt thou return." (Gen 3:19)

> "All flesh shall perish together, and man shall turn again unto dust." (Job 34:15)

There are other verses that suggest a connection between the earth and its inhabitants:

> "Give ear, O ye heavens, and I will speak; and hear, O earth, the words of my mouth." (Deut 32:1)

> "Hear, O heavens, and give ear, O earth: for the LORD hath spoken, I have nourished and brought up children, and they have rebelled against me." (Isa 1:2)

> "O earth, earth, earth, hear the word of the LORD." (Jer 22:29)

These verses are not talking about the literal earth or heavens hearing, but the occupants of them. Here is another verse:

> "And I saw one of his heads as it were wounded to death; and his deadly wound was healed: and all the world ("ge," *Strong's* NT#1093) wondered after the beast." (Rev 13:3)

It is people who are wondering after the beast, not the world as in the planet. The Greek word "ge" that is here translated "world" – and meaning people - is the same word that is translated "earth" in the phrase "three days and three nights in the heart of the earth."

An Important Clue

We must assume that Jesus had a good reason for using this uncommon wording - "in the heart of the earth" in Matthew 12:40. Perhaps this is a key to help unlock the meaning of this prophecy.

Indeed, in Chapter Six, we will see that in His parables, Jesus frequently used earth, soil, etc. in this way. Could He have been saying in this case, that for the three days and three nights He would not necessarily be in the earth (as in ground or soil), but somehow surrounded, confined, or controlled by the inhabitants of the earth? It seems like a reasonable possibility. However, we first need to resolve the three-days-and-three-nights issue and maybe some other questions.

Jesus said He would be "in the heart of the earth." The words He used, if we look at their Biblical usage, convey the meaning of being in the control of the will (heart, Greek - kardia) of man (earth, Greek - ge). Had He meant to say that He would be buried in the earth or ground, the gospel writers could have reported His words using the Greek word "mesos" meaning middle or midst in a phrase like "midst of the earth," or they could have simply used the word for the grave (Greek mnemeion, *Strong's* NT#3419) as in:

> "The people therefore that was with him when he called Lazarus out of his <u>grave</u> [mnemeion], and raised him from the dead, bare record." (John 12:17)

In summary, there is no Biblical support for "in the heart of the earth," meaning that Jesus was in the center of the earth (as in the ground). There is only human tradition which is sometimes reflected in lexicons and commentaries. However, it must be remembered that these sources are not inspired and may have been affected by their authors' understandings of scripture. That doesn't mean we shouldn't use them, but that we must also examine how the Bible itself uses words. By comparing how original words are used in various contexts we can allow the Bible to "interpret" itself. Obviously, the two important words from the phrase "in the <u>heart</u> of the <u>earth</u>," have different meanings than what most people have understood. These are important clues to lead us to a proper understanding of this subject.

The Start of the Three Days and Three Nights

When do the three days and three nights start, and when do they end? Let's see how Jesus Himself counted the time period. I think we'll find that He was mathematically correct. Consider this scripture:

> "And while they abode in Galilee, Jesus said unto them, The Son of man shall be <u>betrayed into the hands of men</u>: And they shall kill him, and <u>the third day</u> he shall be raised again ..." (Matt 17:22-23)

Before they had even gone to Jerusalem, Jesus told His disciples that He would be betrayed, killed and raised again "the third day." He wasn't referring to Tuesday, the third day of the week. He was using "third" in a relative sense. The question is: Relative to what? What event starts the sequence? Jesus gives a series of events – the betrayal, His death and His resurrection. He said something very similar a few chapters later in Matthew:

"… the Son of man shall be betrayed unto the chief priests and unto the scribes, and they shall condemn him to death. And shall deliver him to the Gentiles to mock and scourge and to crucify *him*; and <u>the third day</u> he shall rise again." (Matt 20:18-19)

The difference is that He gave a more complete sequence of events. In this verse, the Son of man shall be:

1. betrayed;   2. condemned;   3. delivered;   4. mocked;
5. scourged;   6. crucified;   7. raised.

Raised, not on the third day of the week, but raised the third day relative to the starting point of the series of events, which is the betrayal. The angels at the grave said to the women:

"He is not here, but is risen: remember how he spake unto you when he was yet in Galilee, Saying, The Son of man must be delivered into the hands of sinful men, and be crucified, and the third day rise again." (Luke 24:6-7)

Again, the series of events does not begin with Jesus' crucifixion, but with His betrayal. We usually understand that the betrayal was just following the Last Supper on Thursday evening. However, we need to carefully examine every point of scripture. Note that I am here saying that the Last Supper was on Thursday evening. This is the most common understanding and is assumed at this point in this study. Evidence will come to light as we go through the Biblical details to establish the chronology. Matthew 26 records the account of Jesus attending a meal at the house of Simon the leper in Bethany:

"Now when Jesus was in Bethany, in the house of Simon the leper …" (Matt 26:6)

Following the dinner, it says:

"Then one of the twelve, called Judas Iscariot, went unto the chief priests, And said *unto them*, What will ye give me, and I will deliver him unto you? And they covenanted with him for thirty pieces of silver." (Matt 26:14-15)

Mark reports the same incident:

"And Judas Iscariot, one of the twelve, went unto the chief priests, <u>to betray him</u> unto them." (Mark 14:10)

Here is the betrayal! The money has even changed hands. Some might argue that the betrayal only happened in the Garden on Thursday evening. I think either act could be classified as betrayal. We would commonly think of something like Judas' deal with the priests as betrayal even if the handover never actually happened then. Certainly, as Jesus magnified the law to include the intents of the heart (Matt 5:22, 28 etc.) we would count it as a betrayal.

Now, when was that dinner? Just before the meal, it gives us the answer. Jesus said:

> "Ye know that after two days is *the feast of* the Passover, and the Son of man is betrayed to be crucified." (Matt 26:2)

Jesus said it was two days until the Passover and Jesus ate the Passover meal Thursday evening, the evening before His crucifixion:

> "Now the first *day* of the *feast of* unleavened bread the disciples came to Jesus, saying unto Him, Where wilt thou that we prepare for thee <u>to eat the passover</u>? And He said, Go into the city to such a man, and say to Him, The Master saith, My time is at hand: <u>I will keep the passover</u> at thy house with my disciples. And the disciples did as Jesus had appointed them; and they <u>made ready the passover</u>. Now when the even was come, he sat down with the twelve." (Matt 26:17-20)

Since Jesus ate the Passover meal with His disciples on Thursday evening there should be no question which day was Passover.

This shows that the betrayal was initiated two days before the Thursday evening Passover meal and thus on Tuesday evening. Judas then completed the handover of Jesus after the Thursday evening Passover meal (John 13:21-30). The crucifixion occurred the following afternoon.

So Jesus' celebration of the Passover meal with His disciples (what we would call the Last Supper), was on Thursday evening and the dinner at Simon's house was on Tuesday evening, two days before. (The Thursday evening timing for Jesus' observance of the Passover will be covered in more detail in Chapter Four.) The time period therefore starts with the betrayal to the priests on Tuesday evening.

This reckoning of the time will be seen to be consistent with Jesus being "three days and three nights in the heart of the earth."

Again, here is the order of events: betrayed, condemned, delivered, mocked, scourged, crucified and finally resurrected at the end of a period of three days and three nights. There is one verse that refers to the third day without mentioning the betrayal:

> "For I delivered unto you first of all that which I also received, how that Christ died for our sins <u>according to the scriptures</u>; And that he was buried, and that he rose again the third day <u>according to the scriptures</u>:" (1 Cor 15:3-4)

However, Paul is just quoting part of the earlier scriptures referring to Jesus' death. He refers to the third day but qualifies it with the phrase "according to the scriptures." We have to determine when the third day was "according to the scriptures."

The End of the Three Days and Three Nights

The series of events and Jesus' time "in the heart of the earth" would have started with the betrayal after the feast at Simon's house on Tuesday evening. Then when would they have ended? Let's use a diagram to help:

Tuesday		Wednesday		Thursday		Friday		Saturday	
Nisan 12		Nisan 13		Nisan 14/Pass.		Nisan 15/FUB		Nisan 16/FFF	
Third Day		Fourth Day		Fifth Day		Preparation Day		Sabbath Day	
		Night 1	Day 1	Night 2	Day 2	Night 3	Day 3		
	S				P		D R		

Nisan = the first month of the festival year; Pass. = Passover; FUB = Feast of Unleavened Bread; FFF = Feast of First Fruits; S = Simon's feast; P = Passover meal (Jesus' observance); D = death; R = resurrection

The "Feast of Unleavened Bread" and "Feast of First Fruits" and their connection to the Passover will be explained later. Let's now identify the three days and three nights:

> **Night one** was the dark part of Tuesday night and Wednesday morning until sunrise.
>
> **Day one** was the light part of Wednesday until sunset which would mark the beginning of the day of Passover.
>
> **Night two** was the dark part of Wednesday night and Thursday morning until sunrise.
>
> **Day two** was the light part of Thursday during which the lamb was to be killed and prepared for the meal.
>
> **Night three** was the dark part of Thursday night and Friday morning until sunrise. Jesus ate the Passover meal with His disciples in the early hours of Nisan 15. Then He went to Gethsemane and was arrested .
>
> **Day three** was the light part of Friday until sunset. The events included the trials, the scourging, crucifixion and death at about 3 pm and burial before sunset, completing the three days and three nights.

During this time, starting Tuesday evening when the priests had paid the money to Judas, they were going forward with their plans to destroy Jesus as heavenly restraint was removed. Jesus was "in the heart of the earth," in that what was within the heart of man toward Him was being manifested by their actions in paying His betrayer, then plotting and carrying out His death.

The Time Period is Not the Most Important Aspect of the Sign

It should be noted that in the two other passages that relate the sign of Jonah, there is not even a mention of the-three-day-and-three-night time period:

> "A wicked and adulterous generation seeketh after a sign; and there shall no sign be given unto it, but the sign of the prophet Jonas. And he left them, and departed." (Matt 16:4)

> "And when the people were gathered thick together, he began to say, This is an evil generation: they seek a sign; and there shall no sign be given it, but the sign of Jonas the prophet. For as Jonas was a sign unto the Ninevites, so shall also the Son of man be to this generation. … The men of Nineve shall rise up in the judgment with this generation, and shall condemn it: for they repented at the preaching of Jonas; and, behold, a greater than Jonas *is* here." (Luke 11:29-30, 32)

Since these verses do not even mention the time period, it would seem most unlikely that the key factor was the exact length of time, or even the time at all. It was more likely the reaction of the people and their actions toward Jesus as compared to the reaction of the people of Nineveh to the preaching of Jonah (Matt 12:41). We will see in Chapter Six, that rather than the time period of "the three days and three nights," it was Jesus' position of being "in the heart of man" that was the more important part of "the sign of Jonah."

When Pilate finally gave in and turned Jesus over to His enemies it is described as:

> "And he released unto them him that for sedition and murder was cast into prison, whom they had desired; but he delivered Jesus <u>to their will</u>." (Luke 23:25)

"Their will," what was in their heart, was expressed as they and others clamored:

> "… Crucify *him*, crucify him." (Luke 23:21)

> "… His blood *be* on us, and on our children." (Matt 27:25)

The handover of Jesus, by Pilate, would not have been possible if God had not previously withdrawn (to a degree) His protection and allowed Him to be "in the heart of the earth." Jesus had earlier been protected from their murderous designs upon Him:

> "Then they sought to take him: but no man laid hands on him, because his hour was not yet come." (John 7:30)

However, when the hour (time) came, that protection was withdrawn and His enemies began to prevail over Him. Jesus subjected Himself to the will of man but, we understand, He did it willingly. Of course, even with our new understanding that being "in the heart of the earth" really means being in the heart of man, we are still dealing with a figurative reference. Jesus wasn't in the physical heart of a man. It is similar to, for instance, John's description of Satan's state during the millennium:

> "And I saw an angel come down from heaven, having the key of the bottomless pit and a great chain in his hand. And he laid hold on the dragon, that old serpent, which is the Devil, and Satan, and <u>bound him</u> a thousand years." (Rev 20:1-2)

Satan cannot be bound with a physical chain. However, he will be bound by a figurative chain of circumstance. There will be no one to tempt during the millennium because all of the wicked will be slain at the second coming. He could:

"… deceive the nations no more, till the thousand years should be fulfilled: …"
(Rev 20:3)

Then, at the end of the millennium, the resurrection of the wicked figuratively looses him; it allows him to once again go forth to tempt them. (Rev 20:7-8)

> While we need to recognize that even the Bible uses figures of speech, we also need to use the Bible to help determine their correct meaning.

Going back to Jesus' situation, we now have a sense in which Jesus was within the heart of man. We also have Biblical evidence for the beginning and ending points of the time period of three days and three nights. This solves the three-days-and-three-nights problem but creates another one.

The new problem is that the period of three days and three nights, starting Tuesday evening, would end right at the beginning of the Sabbath on Friday evening. What does this mean? Jesus would have to escape or somehow be released from His confinement "in the heart of the earth" – the control of man - right at the start of the Sabbath. In some way, He would be no longer be subject to the control of man. It could be reasoned that that was accomplished by His death. We use the expression that death is "a sweet release" in the sense that it is a release from the suffering and difficulties of this life. His death then, sometime before sunset on Friday, would end the time period of three days and three nights. This allows for the resurrection to occur at, or anytime after the start of the Sabbath since, as we have seen, being in the heart of the earth is actually not referring to being in the grave anyway.

We will see, as we go on in this study, that there are clues in the Bible to reveal the real timing of the resurrection that many people have not considered before.

Chapter 3 – His Resurrection on the Lord's Day

In this chapter, we will find the answers to three important questions in relation to the resurrection.

Question 1: When Does the Bible Say the Resurrection Occurred?

In Chapter Two, we found that "in the heart of the earth" means something quite different than what most people have always understood. We also discovered a problem with the idea that Jesus was in the grave for three days and three nights. It was proposed that the time period was actually referring to the time Jesus was, in a sense, in the control of man and subject to man's will and that the time period ended likely at the time of His death. In this chapter, we will discover a translation problem that few people are aware of, and a solution that will suggest a different timing for Jesus' resurrection than what is normally understood.

Question 2: How Did "Thine Holy One" Not "See Corruption"?

Peter, speaking of David's prophecy of Christ (" … neither wilt thou suffer thine Holy One to see corruption." Psalm 16:10), said:

> "He [David] seeing this before spake of the resurrection of Christ, that his soul was not left in hell, neither his flesh did see corruption." (Acts 2:31)

This verse is saying that Jesus' body would not see corruption or experience decay. However, it is well known that, after death, a body will quickly start to decompose. The whole (modern) embalming process is done so that a body can be presentable at a funeral a few days after death.

> It was important that no taint of decay come upon the Holy One of God Who showed us everything that was good about God.

If Jesus was in the grave from His burial late Friday afternoon until a Sunday-morning resurrection, His body would surely have begun to decay. Some might reason that God miraculously prevented His body from decaying in order to fulfill the prophecy. However, God gives predictions for specific and significant reasons – not just to have fulfilled predictions. Is it possible that it was given because God's intent was to raise Jesus to life before there was time for decay to start?

This was in contrast to the resurrection of Lazarus who did see corruption:

"Jesus said, Take ye away the stone. Martha, the sister of him that was dead, saith unto him, Lord, by this time he stinketh: for he hath been *dead* four days." (John 11:39)

Christ did not see corruption. Lazarus, resurrection was described as:

" … he that was dead came forth, bound hand and foot with graveclothes: and his face was bound about with a napkin …" (John 11:44)

The graveclothes are associated with corruption and mortality. Our Lord was raised from the dead in incorruption and immortality. His first and subsequent post-resurrection appearances were without graveclothes.

So again, the question is: with a Friday afternoon burial and a Sunday morning resurrection how was the decay of Jesus' body prevented?

Question 3: How Was the Passover Lamb Not to be Left Until Morning?

Here is another thought related to the timing: when the Passover lamb was sacrificed and prepared for the Passover meal, it was to be eaten that evening and any part left over was to be burned so that nothing remained of it in the morning:

"And ye shall let nothing of it remain until the morning; and that which remaineth of it until the morning ye shall burn with fire." (Exo 12:10)

The idea was that the sacrifice was complete with nothing left of it by morning. This suggests a problem with the idea that the slain body of Jesus, the true Passover Lamb, was remaining the morning after the crucifixion.

> Sacrificial lambs were not to be left until the morning,
> and this was done in order to prevent any corruption.

When Abraham was directed to sacrifice his only son Isaac, foreshadowing Jesus' death, he was told not just to slay him but to:

"… offer him there for a burnt offering upon one of the mountains which I will tell thee of." (Gen 22:2)

He was to slay his son and offer him as a "burnt offering" thus fulfilling the requirements for a sacrifice. The point here is that there was to be nothing left of a sacrifice by morning; nothing that could see corruption. Of course, corruption was synonymous with sin.

In the case of the Passover Lamb, whatever could not be consumed was to be burned indicating a complete sacrifice. There is a problem here with the traditional understanding of Jesus' fulfillment of the specifications for the Passover sacrifice, because in that understanding He was still remaining in the morning; His body had not been completely consumed. John describes the breaking of the legs of the thieves and how Jesus' legs were not broken, and then says:

"For these things were done, that the scripture should be fulfilled, A bone of him shall not be broken." (John 19:36)

The scripture that was being fulfilled was:

"They shall leave none of it unto the morning, nor break any bone of it: according to all the ordinances of the passover they shall keep it." (Num 9:12)

We tend to focus on the fulfillment of the fact that no bone of Jesus would be broken, however this scripture also includes the specification that: "They shall leave none of it unto the morning." Shouldn't this part of the prophecy have been equally fulfilled? How was it fulfilled? For it to be fulfilled His body should have been burned so that nothing would be left of it until morning. To be remaining in a tomb the next morning (never mind somewhere close to three days later), would not seem to fulfill the requirements.

Where else in scripture is a sacrificial animal ever buried? It is never recorded. To bury would be to subject it to decay. Part of the whole point of having a lamb without blemish was to illustrate perfection. Is there another way in which none of this ultimate sacrifice could be left until morning to decay? This study will answer that question too.

The Bible Says "Sabbaton"

Now we will again look into the original meanings of some key words to find answers to these questions. We should not be afraid to question our understanding of scripture as we attempt to establish every point. As mentioned earlier, there is a little-known problem with the translation of some key words in the King James Bible and other versions. A correct understanding will answer all of these questions. If you have a problem with the thought that there could be translation errors, please keep reading and take the time to read *Appendix 3 – Some Thoughts About Inspiration*, p. 122. Also remember that, while God's original word is inspired, the punctuation and all later translations and versions are the work of man.

> Anyone could take the time to write their own version of the Bible and do the best job they could. That would not make their work inspired.

If you compare the original Greek wording in an interlinear version of the Bible, you will find that the references to the first day of the week as resurrection morning actually use the Greek word "Sabbaton," commonly meaning the seventh-day Sabbath. It does not mean, in today's common usage, Sunday, the first day of the week, even though that is how it has been translated in a few Bible passages. Sabbaton is the Greek word for Sabbath the seventh day of the week, Saturday in the English language, and similar words in many other languages. Here are some examples among many:

Al Sabit - Arabic	Shapat - Armenian
Sabuatu - Assyrian	Sobota – Bohemian, Polish
Samedi - French	Sabbaton - Greek
Shabat – Hebrew	Sabtu – Indonesian
Sabado - Portuguese, Spanish, Tagalog	Sabatico – Prussian
Subbota – Russian	Shabes - Yiddish

The Greek word "sabbaton" (*Strong's* NT#4521) is used in the New Testament 68 times. Fifty-nine times it is translated as "Sabbath" or "Sabbath day" as it is commonly understood. However, in the other nine uses, the very same original word is translated "week" as in the phrase "first day of the week." Here is the *Online Bible Greek Lexicon* entry showing the various meanings for sabbaton:

1) the seventh day of each week which was a sacred festival on which the Israelites were required to abstain from all work
   1a) the institution of the sabbath, the law for keeping holy every seventh day of the week
   1b) a single sabbath, sabbath day
2) seven days, a week

Six of the nine cases where it is translated as "week" are in reference to the resurrection, two refer to religious gatherings and one is in reference to fasting. Let's take a careful look at each of these and see if, in their context, they could logically have been referring not to the first day of the week but to the Sabbath.

Common Usage of "Sabbaton"

First, let's see how it is most commonly and correctly used. In the following and all subsequent interlinear examples, the Greek appears first, followed by the English word-for-word translation below each line of Greek. Finally, the King James Version is shown. The Greek word we know as "Sabbaton" is underlined. (Interlinear text material, in each case, is from Jay P. Green, *Pocket Interlinear New Testament, 1982*):

> ανασπασει   αυτον   εν   τη ημερα   του   <u>σαββατον</u>
> **he will pull up   it   on   the day   of the   sabbath**
> "And answered them, saying, Which of you shall have an ass or an ox fallen into a pit, and will not straightway <u>pull him out on the sabbath day</u>?" (Luke 14:5)

This verse is very clearly referring to the seventh-day Sabbath. No one would argue with that. Since we are going to look at a number of verses like this, it might help in this study to learn at least a few letters of Greek. The word sabbaton in Greek is spelled: **σαββατων.** The last few letters of the word will vary a little depending on the tense and whether the use is singular or plural, but at least learn to recognize the "sabba" portion:

σ = sigma
α = alpha
β = beta
β = beta
α = alpha

It is interesting to note the similarity between the word Sabbath and the word abba, which means father.

Here are some further examples of the common usage of sabbaton:

ην   γαρ   μεγαλη   η   ημερα   εκεινου του   <u>**σαββατον**</u>
was for   great   the   day   of that   sabbath
"The Jews therefore, because it was the preparation, that the bodies should not remain upon the cross on the sabbath day, (<u>for that sabbath day was an high day,</u>) besought Pilate that their legs might be broken, and *that* they might be taken away." (John 19:31)

αγανακτων   οτι τω   <u>**σαββατω**</u>   θεραπευσενο ιησους
being angry   that on   the Sabbath   healed   Jesus
"And the ruler of the synagogue answered <u>with indignation, because that Jesus had healed on the sabbath</u> day, and said unto the people, There are six days in which men ought to work: in them therefore come and be healed, and not on the sabbath day." (Luke 13:14)

τουτου τη   ημερα του   <u>**σαββατον**</u>
this   the   day   of the   sabbath
"And ought not this woman, being a daughter of Abraham, whom Satan hath bound, lo, these eighteen years, be loosed from <u>this bond on the sabbath day</u>?" (Luke 13:16)

All of these texts are clearly referring to the seventh-day Sabbath, and in each, the Greek word sabbaton is correctly translated as "Sabbath."

Resurrection Texts

There are six verses in the King James Version, referring to the resurrection, that contain the phrase "first day of the week." In each of these cases, not only is the Greek word "sabbaton" translated as "week" but the word "day" is supplied; it is not in the original at all. (In most editions of the

King James Bible supplied words are printed in italics.) Also, in five cases the Greek word for "one" is translated as "first." Something strange has happened in the translation process. Here are the verses in question:

> "In the end of the sabbath, as it began to dawn toward the <u>first *day* of the week</u>, came Mary Magdalene and the other Mary to see the sepulchre." (Matt 28:1)

> "And very early in the morning the <u>first *day* of the week</u>, they came unto the sepulchre at the rising of the sun." (Mark 16:2)

> "Now when *Jesus* was risen early the <u>first *day* of the week</u>, he appeared first to Mary Magdalene, out of whom he had cast seven devils." (Mark 16:9)

> "Now upon the <u>first *day* of the week</u>, very early in the morning, they came unto the sepulchre, bringing the spices which they had prepared, and certain *others* with them." (Luke 24:1)

> "The <u>first *day* of the week</u> cometh Mary Magdalene early, when it was yet dark, unto the sepulchre, and seeth the stone taken away from the sepulchre." (John 20:1)

> "Then the same day at evening, being the <u>first *day* of the week</u>, when the doors were shut where the disciples were assembled for fear of the Jews, came Jesus and stood in the midst, and saith unto them, Peace *be* unto you." (John 20:19)

Let's carefully look at how this phrase "the first day of the week" is used in these verses. The first verse that we will start with is from Luke:

> **Τη δε μια των σαββατων ορθρου**
> **The but one of the week while still**
> **βαθεος ηλθον επι το μνημαα**
> **very early they came on the tomb**
> Now upon the <u>first *day* of the week</u>, very early in the morning, they came unto the sepulchre, bringing the spices ..." (Luke 24:1)

In some cases, including the verse above, the interlinear version even shows the word for word translation of "sabbaton" as week.

The same Greek words used in Luke 4:16 to say that Jesus stood up to read "on the Sabbath" are used here in reference to the resurrection, to say that Jesus was raised on "the first day of the week."

Here are some translations that render the Greek words closer to their original meanings:

"Now in the early depths of <u>one of the sabbaths</u>, they, and certain others together with them, came to the tomb, bringing the spices which they make ready."
(Luke 24:1, *The Concordant Literal New Testament*)

"And on the <u>first of the sabbaths</u>, at early dawn, they came to the tomb, bearing the spices they made ready, and certain *others* with them,"
(Luke 24:1, *Young's Literal Translation*)

"And the <u>first of the sabbaths</u>, at early dawn, they came to the tomb, carrying spices which they prepared; and some were with them."
(Luke 24:1, *KJ3 Literal Translation*)

Here is the second verse to consider:

τη   δε   <u>μια</u> <u>των</u> <u>σαββατων</u> Μαρια   η   Μαγδαληνη
on the and   first of the Sabbaths   Mary   the Magdalene
ερχεται πρωι σκοτιας ετι ουσης εις τομ ννημειον
comes early, darkness yet being to the   tomb
The <u>first *day* of the week</u> cometh Mary Magdalene early, when it was yet dark, unto the sepulchre, and seeth the stone taken away from the sepulchre.
(John 20:1)

Here are three more-literal translations of this verse:

"Now on <u>one of the sabbaths</u>, Miriam Magdalene is coming to the tomb in the morning, there being still darkness ..."
(John 20:1, *The Concordant Literal New Testament*)

"And on the <u>first of the sabbaths</u>, Mary the Magdalene doth come early (there being yet darkness) to the tomb, and she seeth the stone having been taken away out of the tomb," (John 20:1, *Young's Literal Translation*)

"But on the <u>first of the sabbaths</u>, Mary Magdalene came early in the morning to the tomb, it yet being dark. And she sees the stone having been taken away from the tomb."
(John 20:1, *KJ3 Literal Translation*)

These translations are closer to the meaning of the original wording.

> There is no scriptural evidence whatsoever for the translation
> "first day of the week" in verses referring to the resurrection.

"'One of the sabbaths' is the true rendering. The usual 'first day of the week' is absolutely devoid of scriptural evidence." (*Concordant Commentary,* p. 172)

The Scriptures, a Messianic translation, renders this verse as:

"And on the first day of the week Miryam from Magdala came early to the tomb, while it was still dark, and saw that the stone had been removed from the tomb." (John 20:1, *The Scriptures*)

However, it also includes an explanatory note:

"First Day of the week: The underlying Greek text is 'mia ton sabbaton', which when literally translated means 'one of the sabbath/s', but is <u>traditionally rendered</u> as 'first day of the week. The term 'first day of the week' is literally translated as 'prote hemera tis hebdomata' in Greek, but nowhere appears as such in the N.T." (*The Scriptures*, p. 1214)

It then goes on to say that they have chosen to retain the translation "first day of the week" as it is "traditionally rendered." There are probably no Bible translations that are not influenced by tradition!

The third verse we want to look at is:

> ουσης ουν οψιας τη ημερα εκεινη τη
> **It being then evening day on that the**
> <u>μια</u> <u>των</u> <u>σαββατων</u> και των θυρων
> **first of the Sabbaths and the doors**
> "Then the same day at evening, being the <u>first *day* of</u>
> <u>the week</u>, when the doors were shut …" (John 20:19)

The three verses considered above, in the English, are using the word sabbaton with a meaning quite different from its original. This is done in almost all other English versions of the Bible. The remaining three texts are the same idea, but something quite interesting happens in the case of Matthew 28:1.

> οψε δε σββατων τη επιψωσκουση
> **late in but the week at the dawning**
> εις <u>μιαν</u> <u>σαββατων</u>
> **into the first of the week**
> "In the end of the sabbath, <u>as</u> it began to dawn toward the <u>first *day* of the week</u>, came Mary Magdalene and the other Mary to see the sepulchre." (Matt 28:1)

Do you see a logical problem with this verse as it reads in English directly from the King James Version? The word "as" indicates that two events are happening at the same time. The problem is the way it is translated; the "as" in this verse indicates that the end of the Sabbath is happening as the first day of the week is dawning.

When is the <u>end</u> of the Sabbath? – sunset Saturday.

When is the <u>dawning</u> of the first day of the week? – sunrise Sunday morning.

How far apart are sunset and sunrise? – 12 hours.

How can the Sabbath be ending (at sunset Saturday) as dawn (sunrise) is happening on the first day of the week? The end of the Sabbath and the dawn of the first day of the week are 12 hours apart! You may spot another problem with the translation of this verse which will be discussed later.

The phrase "in the end of the sabbath" uses the Greek word "opse" (*Strong's* NT#3796) which some versions translate as "after" rather than "end:"

> "Now <u>after</u> the Sabbath, near dawn of the first day of the week, Mary of Magdala and the other Mary went to take a look at the tomb."
> (Matt 28:1, *Amplified Bible*)

> "<u>After</u> the Sabbath, at dawn on the first day of the week, Mary Magdalene and the other Mary went to look at the tomb." (Matt 28:1, *New International Version*)

> "Now <u>after</u> the Sabbath, as it began to dawn toward the first day of the week, Mary Magdalene and the other Mary came to look at the grave."
> (Matt 28:1 *New American Standard Bible*)

Thayer studied the use of "after" for the translation of "opse" in Matthew 28:1 and concluded "... an examination of the instances just cited (and others) will show that they fail to sustain the rendering after ..." (*Thayer's Greek Lexicon of the New Testament*, p. 471)

> It is useful to look at how other verses use an original
> word to help determine its meaning.

The original word "opse" is used two other times in the New Testament:

> "And when <u>even</u> was come, he went out of the city." (Mark 11:19)

> "Watch ye therefore: for ye know not when the master of the house cometh, at <u>even</u>, or at midnight, or at the cockcrowing, or in the morning:" (Mark 13:35)

In these verses, it is translated as "even." With the idea of evening and morning making up a day, the evening is the dark part of the Sabbath. In Matthew 28:1, it could therefore have the meaning "during the dark part of the Sabbath just as it is beginning to get light," which agrees with the next part of the verse "as it began to dawn," or grow light shortly before sunrise.

Here are some more-correct, literal, English translations:

"Now it is the <u>evening of the sabbaths</u>. At the lighting up [dawn] into one of the sabbaths came Mary Magdalene and the other Mary to behold the sepulcher."
(Matt 28:1, *The Concordant Literal New Testament*)

"And on the <u>eve of the sabbaths</u>, at the dawn, toward the first of the sabbaths, came Mary the Magdalene, and the other Mary, to see the sepulchre,"
(Matt 28:1, *Young's Literal Translation*)

"But <u>late in the sabbaths</u>, at the dawning into the first of the sabbaths, Mary the Magdalene and the other Mary came to gaze upon the grave."
(Matt 28:1, *KJ3 Literal Translation*)

The remaining two verses where sabbaton is translated as "week" are:

"And very early in the morning the <u>first *day* of the week</u>, they came unto the sepulchre at the rising of the sun." (Mark 16:2)

"Now when *Jesus* was risen early the <u>first *day* of the week</u>, he appeared first to Mary Magdalene, out of whom he had cast seven devils." (Mark 16:9)

These verses have the same translation issues as described above. Here they are from a more-literal version:

"and early in the morning of the <u>first of the sabbaths</u>, they come unto the sepulchre, at the rising of the sun," (Mark 16:2, *Young's Literal Translation*)

"And he, having risen in the morning of the <u>first of the sabbaths</u>, did appear first to Mary the Magdalene, out of whom he had cast seven demons;"
(Mark 16:9, *Young's Literal Translation*)

The verse before Mark 16:2 needs to be examined because, in the King James Version, it suggests that the Sabbath has ended:

"And when the sabbath was past, Mary Magdalene, and Mary the *mother* of James, and Salome, had bought sweet spices, that they might come and anoint him." (Mark 16:1)

However, other versions translate it in a way consistent with the understanding given here of the meaning of verse 2, and the timing of the events of the resurrection:

"And, for the elapsing of the sabbath, Mary Magdalene and Mary the mother of James, and Salome, buy spices, that, coming, they should be rubbing Him."
(Mark 16:1, *The Concordant Literal New Testament*)

The meaning then is that, since the Sabbath was about to start, they bought the spices and very early the next morning they came to the sepulchre. Mark 16:9 actually uses the Greek word protos which means "first" and therefore the phrase translated as "first day of the week" actually means "first Sabbath" as sabbaton, in this case, is singular and "day" is a supplied word.

This quote, from the *Concordant Commentary*, shows that some Greek scholars recognize the problems in the common translations of these verses:

> "The resurrection did not occur on Sunday, or 'the first day of the week,' but on the first one of the seven sabbaths which led from Firstfruits to Pentecost. The notable phrase 'one of the sabbaths' is always found in the interval between Passover and Pentecost, never at any other time of the year. It may refer to any sabbath of the seven. It is usually used of the resurrection day (Mt. 28:1, Mk. 16:1-2, Jn. 20:1-19), which would be during the days of unleavened bread, but also of a sabbath after this (Ac. 20:6,7), any time up to Pentecost (1 Co. 16:2,8). Scholars are divided as to the reason for the rendering 'first day of the week.' It was usual to say that 'one' is sometimes used for *first,* and that 'sabbaths' sometimes means week, but the latest attempts to justify the accepted rendering is that 'one of the sabbaths' is equivalent to 'the first day *after* the sabbath.' As the day after the sabbath was commonly called the 'morrow of the sabbath' (Lev. 23:15,LXX), this seems far-fetched. Even if we take 'one' to mean first in this case, the sense is not changed for the first of a series of sabbaths, as we read in Mark 16:9. But in no case was sabbaths ever used for 'week'. That is always represented by hebdomad, or seven. The only exception would be when a number of sabbaths measure the same space of time as so many hebdomads. As the expression 'first day of the week' can be so readily expressed in Greek there are grave grounds for refusing to use these words as the equivalent of 'one of the sabbaths.'" *(Concordant Commentary, p. 136)*

It is obvious that when the phrase "first day of the week," as used in reference to the resurrection, is carefully examined there are serious problems with the way it has been translated.

> Not everyone accepts the traditional belief that
> Jesus rose from the dead on a Sunday morning.

Verses Concerning Spiritual Meetings

Now let's look at the two verses where "sabbaton" is translated as "week" in the context of a religious meeting. Acts 20:7 says, in the King James Version, that the disciples came together on the first day of the week, yet the original Greek says that it was on the Sabbath.

εν δε τη μια των σαββατων συνηγμενων
on and the one of the sabbaths having been assembled
"And upon the <u>first *day* of the week</u>, when the disciples came together to break bread, Paul preached unto them, ready to depart on the morrow; and continued his speech until midnight." (Acts 20:7)

Greek experts Robert K. Brown and Philip W. Comfort in the *New Greek English Interlinear New Testament* translate this verse as:

> "And on one of the Sabbaths having been assembled us to break bread, Paul was lecturing them ..." (Acts 20:7, *New Greek English Interlinear New Testament*)

In 1 Corinthians 16:2 there has been a similar change from the Greek word "sabbaton" to the English word "week:"

> **κατα   μιαν σαββατων εκαστος υμων παρ εαυτω τιθετω**
> **every one of a week   each   of you by himself let him put**
> "Upon the <u>first *day* of the week</u> let every one of you lay by him in store, as
> *God* hath prospered him, that there be no gatherings when I come."
> (1 Cor 16:2)

> We can see an attempt, in history, to put more emphasis
> on Sunday, the first day of the week.

A more literal translations is:

> "On the first of the sabbaths, let each one of you put by himself, storing up
> whatever he is prospered, that there not be collections when I come."
> (1 Cor 16:2, *KJ3 Literal Translation*)

A Word Study of "First Day of the Week"

The word "first" in this phrase comes from the Greek word "mia" (*Strong's* NT#3391). The word means and is most commonly translated (62 times in the King James Version) as "one." There are eight instances where it is translated as "first," and it is interesting to note, all but one of these are in verses referring to the resurrection.

Of course, the word "day" in this phrase is not translated from a Greek word at all. It is supplied by the translators and does not even appear in the original.

If one wishes to say "first day" in Greek, there are specific words to do so. The word for "first" in Greek is "protos" (*Strong's* NT#4413). The word for "day" in Greek is "hemera" (*Strong's* NT#2250). Here are two examples of the use of the phrase "first day" that use "protos" and "hemera":

> "And the <u>first day</u> of unleavened bread, when they killed the passover, his disciples said unto him, Where wilt thou that we go and prepare that thou mayest eat the passover?" (Mark 14:12)

"For your fellowship in the gospel from the <u>first day</u> until now;" (Phil 1:5)

So if one wishes to say "first day" in Greek, the words are "protos hemera," not "mia Sabbaton" which, literally translated, means more like "one Sabbath" or "one of the Sabbaths."

There is a Greek word for "week" which is "hebdomad" and means "week" or "sevens." In the New Testament, this Greek word is never used. The English word "week" only appears in the King James Version translated from the Greek word "sabbaton."

In summary, the changes in original word meanings that were made within this one phrase are:

> The word "mia" which means "one," was translated as "first."
> The word "day," which is not even in the original was added.
> The word "sabbaton," which means "Sabbath" was translated as "week."

As the expression "first day of the week" is easy to express in Greek,
there is no reason to twist meanings and add words to come up with it.

These changes resulted in a change from the obvious, more literal meaning, "one of the sabbaths," to "first day of the week." Between this and having a correct understanding of "in the heart of the earth," we have some good clues to correctly understand Jesus' use of this phrase.

Word Genders

In Greek, and in many other languages, the genders of a noun and its modifying adjective or definite article must match. An example of this that we are familiar with in English is the borrowed Spanish term "el niño" which we use to refer to a certain climatic pattern that often occurs in the Pacific Ocean. It actually has reference to "the little boy" referring to Jesus who, tradition says, was born about the time of year (Christmas) that this climate pattern is observed off the west coast of Spanish-speaking South America. In this case, the masculine adjective "el" modifies niño. Similarly, the feminine adjective "la" modifies the feminine word "niña" giving us "la niña" meaning "the little girl."

Since the Greek word "mia" or "mian" (meaning "one," not "first") is in the feminine gender and the Greek word for Sabbath, "Sabbaton," is neuter gender, the phrase mia sabbaton cannot simply be translated "one of the Sabbaths" because the genders for the two words don't match. And so we have a problem.

The solution the translators used was to add the feminine word "hemera" (day, *Strong's* NT#2250) which, they must have reasoned, was implied (as it certainly is), and to translate the feminine word "mia" (*Strong's* NT#3391) as "first." Then the genders of "mia" and "hemera," both feminine words, match, and with the (mis)translation of "sabbaton" (*Strong's* NT#4521) into "week," we end up with translations such as:

> "And very early in the morning
> the <u>first</u>   (meaning changed)
> <u>*day*</u>   (word added)
> of the <u>week</u>,   (meaning changed)
> they came unto the sepulchre at
> the rising of the sun." (Mark 16:2)

You can verify this by checking Mark 16:2 in an interlinear Bible - you will see that there is no word for "day" in the original Greek. Of course, "first day of the sabbath" doesn't make sense. But then the translators gave a totally different meaning to the Greek word "Sabbaton" (Sabbath) by translating it into the word "week." As we are discovering, in this investigation, there is no justification for doing this.

What a twisted way to make a translation! There is another, simpler and better way to do this. The word "day," admittedly implied, could just as easily be added after the word "sabbath." In fact, the King James Bible does add the word "day" after "sabbath" many times. In Matthew 12 itself, this is done seven times. Here is the first example:

> "At that time Jesus went on the sabbath <u>day</u> through the corn; and his disciples were an hungred, and began to pluck the ears of corn, and to eat." (Matt 12:1)

However, since the word "day" is implied it doesn't even have to be included to take care of the gender issue. Some Bible versions do this and retain the original meaning:

> "And, very early in the morning on
> one   (original meaning retained)
> of the sabbaths,   (original meaning retained, "day" implied)
> they are coming to the tomb at
> the rising of the sun." (Mark 16:2, *The Concordant Literal New Testament*)

> "And early in the morning of the first of the sabbaths, they come unto the sepulchre, at the rising of the sun," (Mark 16:2, *Young's Literal Translation*)

> To correctly understand the Bible, sometimes we have to investigate
> even minor items like word genders. Bible study takes effort!

Can you see how the translation as done in the King James Version and most other modern translations would change people's understanding of the truth? This is another major clue to help us correctly understand the true meaning of the passage in Matthew 12.

A Verse Concerning Fasting

The last of the seven verses concerns fasting and, again, "sabbaton" is translated into week:

νηστευω δις τον σαββατον
I fast   twice   in the week,
"I fast twice <u>in the week</u>, I give tithes of all that I possess." (Luke 18:12)

Why was it translated this way? One might argue that it's impossible to fast twice in one day, so the reference must be to two fasts in one week. But that is imposing an interpretation before we have even translated the words! Better to translate the words and then attempt to discern the meaning. Also, who says that a fast must be a full 24 hours or more? Isn't it possible that a person could fast twice in one day, for instance, by skipping two meals? Our understanding of fasting does not justify changing the meaning from "Sabbath" to "week." Here are some translations that are closer to the original word meanings:

> "I fast twice *on* the sabbath; I tithe things, as many as I get."
> (Luke 18:12, *KJ3 Literal Translation*)

> "I fast twice *on* the Sabbath, I give tithes of all that I possess."
> (Luke 18:12, *Modern King James Bible*)

Sabbaton Means Sabbath

In the Greek phrase "μια των σαββάτων" which literally translates "one of the sabbaths," the word "σαββάτων" is plural. Grammatically, it doesn't make sense to translate it as the singular word "week." This only adds to the problem of taking a word that has a particular meaning and assigning it a totally different meaning! There is no support for the idea that the phrase should be translated as "first day of the week." This is done purely on the basis of tradition, in support of Sunday sacredness and with no Biblical basis whatsoever.

We have carefully examined the nine verses in which the King James Bible translators have rendered "Sabbaton" as "week." In every case, there is good evidence for translating it according to its correct meaning as "Sabbath" as is done in the 59 other cases of its use. It is better to faithfully translate the words, and then derive our theology, rather than to twist the meanings of words to match our theology. The evidence above shows that the resurrection verses considered could reasonably have been translated another way - a way that is more consistent with the original word meanings.

Summary

In Chapter Two, we saw that the three days and three nights extended from Tuesday evening to Friday afternoon. In this chapter we have learned that the verses saying He arose on the first day of the week should be translated more like "on the sabbath" or "the first/one of the sabbaths." Now we can consider the possibility of a Friday evening resurrection, early on Sabbath. Since

Jesus is Lord of the Sabbath and the Sabbath is the Lord's Day, it wouldn't be unreasonable for Him to have risen on His day:

"For the Son of man is Lord even of the sabbath day." (Matt 12:8)

> If someone says to you that Jesus rose from the dead on the Lord's Day you can agree with them, no problem.

Most Christians understand that the resurrection must have been on the "first day of the week" to fulfill Jesus' prediction of being dead for "three days and three nights" (i.e. Friday crucifixion and Sunday resurrection). But we have seen, by carefully examining the phrases "three days and three nights," and "in the heart of the earth," that there is a better way to understand it; a way that is more consistent with what the Bible writers actually wrote. Jesus Himself always started His references to the three days and three nights, or similar expressions, with the betrayal, not with His death. Jesus was not dead during those three days and three nights. He was figuratively surrounded by and in the control of His enemies, the inhabitants of the earth, but He was not dead, just as Jonah wasn't dead in the belly of the whale. Jesus was in the "heart of the earth" because He had been given into the heart or will of man for them to do with Him as they pleased. The time period started Tuesday evening and ended either at His death Friday afternoon, or right at the start of the Sabbath, with His resurrection on the Lord's Day. Such a scenario nicely answers the three questions posed at the start of this chapter. Let's review the questions and summarize the findings:

1. When does the Bible say the resurrection occurred? It occurred on the seventh-day Sabbath. We will see more evidence that it was very early on the Sabbath, shortly after sunset.
2. How did God's Holy One not see corruption? He was resurrected shortly after His burial and within a few hours of death. There was hardly time for His body to even cool.
3. How was the Passover Lamb not to be left until morning? He was resurrected before the morning ever came. The tomb was empty.

We have yet to work out the finer details of the timing of the resurrection. As everything needs to fit into the timing of the feasts which had, for centuries, pointed forward to Jesus' death and resurrection, we will now look into that topic.

Chapter 4 – The Timing of the Spring Feasts

The feasts appointed by God in the books of Moses were very important events in the lives of the Israelites. At specified times each spring and fall they were required to assemble at Jerusalem for holy convocations or assemblies before God. The Spring Feasts were all connected to each other, with their beginning point being determined by the new moon and the spring equinox. While the timing of the start of the spring feasts is beyond the topic of this book, we do want to understand the relationship between the different spring feasts as it needs to fit with the timing of Jesus' death and resurrection. The spring feasts, in many ways, foreshadowed the events of Jesus' first coming. The spring feasts consisted of:

1. Passover, Nisan 14, the day when the lamb was to be sacrificed.
2. The Feast of Unleavened Bread including the seven days from Nisan 15 to Nisan 21. During these seven days they were to eat no leavened bread.
3. The Feast of First Fruits, the day on which the wave sheaf of first fruits was presented in recognition of God's providence. The correct timing has been much disputed.
4. Pentecost is best known for the outpouring of the Holy Spirit upon the infant Christian church. Pentecost was 50 days inclusive from the Feast of First Fruits and therefore it would occur on the same day of the week as that feast.

Passover

Nisan was the first month of the religious year and the fourteenth day was designated as the Passover day.

> "Speak ye unto all the congregation of Israel, saying, In the tenth *day* of this month they shall take to them every man a lamb, according to the house of *their* fathers, a lamb for an house: ... And ye shall keep it up until the fourteenth day of the same month: and the whole assembly of the congregation of Israel shall kill it in the evening." (Exo 12:3,6)

> Nisan, the first month of the religious year, was also called Abib meaning "month of the ears" in reference to the developing ears of grain in the spring.

The marginal note in the *Authorized King James Version* says for evening (verse 6): "between the two evenings." More-literal translations give it more directly:

> "And it hath become a charge to you, until the fourteenth day of this month, and the whole assembly of the company of Israel have slaughtered it between the evenings;" (Exo 12:6, *Young's Literal Translation*)

Several versions use the phrase "<u>at the going down of the sun</u>." Of course, the sun would begin it's descent in the sky at noon and continue until sunset. This is the time referred to as "between the evenings."

> "Within the Temple, the day was divided into quarters. The quarter between 12:00 noon and 3:00 pm was called the minor evening oblation, while that between 3:00 pm and 6:00 pm was called the major evening oblation. Therefore, 'between the evenings' means between those two periods or 3:00 pm."
> (Joseph Good, *Rosh HaShanah and the Messianic Kingdom to Come*, p. 20)

The Israelites would keep the lamb from the tenth of Nisan to the fourteenth and then, on the afternoon of the fourteenth, as the sun was descending in the sky, they were to kill it. The lamb was to be "roast with fire" (Exo 12:8) and prepared to be eaten after sunset which marks the start of the next day, Nisan 15 and the beginning of the seven-day Feast of Unleavened Bread. The middle of the between-the-evenings time period would be the middle of the afternoon, about 3 pm which, we understand, was the time of day that Jesus died. Then, after sunset and in the early hours of Nisan 15 they would have the Passover meal that had been prepared on the fourteenth. The following verses help with this understanding:

> "And they shall eat the flesh <u>in that night</u>, roast with fire, and <u>unleavened bread</u>; *and* with bitter *herbs* they shall eat it." (Exo 12:8)

> "In the <u>fourteenth *day*</u> of the first month at even *is* the LORD'S <u>passover</u>. And on the <u>fifteenth day</u> of the same month *is* the [first day of the] <u>feast of unleavened bread</u> unto the LORD: seven days ye must eat unleavened bread." (Lev 23:5-6)

> "And they departed from Rameses in the first month, on the fifteenth day of the first month; on the morrow after the <u>passover</u> the children of Israel went out with an high hand in the sight of all the Egyptians." (Num 33:3)

Factors in the Timing of Passover Observance

There are two things that we need to understand about the timing of Passover observance that become important in this study. The following passage could be confusing because it talks of preparing for the Passover (Nisan 14) on "the first day of the feast of unleavened bread" (Nisan 15):

> "Now <u>the first *day* of the *feast of* unleavened bread</u> the disciples came to Jesus, saying unto him, Where wilt thou that we <u>prepare for thee to eat the passover</u>? And he said, Go into the city to such a man, and say unto him, The Master saith, My time is at hand; I will keep the passover at thy house with my disciples. And the disciples did as Jesus had appointed them; and they made ready the passover. Now when the even was come, he sat down with the twelve." (Matt 26:17-20)

> The Passover meal was eaten in the early evening hours of Nisan 15, technically the first day of the Feast of Unleavened Bread.

First, it is helpful to understand that, by the time of Jesus, the term "Feast of Unleavened Bread" was sometimes used to refer to the whole period of eight days. For instance, the Jewish historian Josephus wrote:

> "Whence it is that, in memory of the want we were then in, we keep a feast for eight days, which is called *the feast of unleavened bread."*
> *(Josephus, Antiquities of the Jews, Book 2, Chapter 15.)*

The eight days would consist of Passover Day followed immediately by the seven days of the Feast of Unleavened Bread. It had come to be considered as one continuous feast and therefore Mark could write:

> "And the first day of unleavened bread, when they killed the passover, his disciples said unto him, Where wilt thou that we go and prepare that thou mayest eat the passover?" (Mark 14:12)

The phrase "when they killed the passover" and the context tell us that the day referred to in the passage above was Nisan 14 even though it was referred to as "the first day of unleavened bread." The disciples clearly understood that Passover was on Thursday with the meal to be observed that evening which would be the early hours of Nisan 15 and the beginning of the Feast of Unleavened Bread.

Second, it helps to clarify the timing of events to understand that <u>Jesus kept the Passover a day before many of the Jews</u>. On Thursday evening, during the meal, Jesus said:

> " … With desire I have desired <u>to eat this passover</u> with you before I suffer:"
> (Luke 22:15)

There is no doubt that Jesus understood this to be the Passover meal. There is no need to look at astronomic tables or other sources to determine Passover timing for that year. Jesus ate with them and then went out to the garden, was taken prisoner by the Jews, endured the various trials early in the morning, was crucified about 9 am and died about 3 pm on Friday afternoon. According to John, at this time, at least some of the Jews had not yet partaken of the Passover:

> "Then led they Jesus from Caiaphas unto the hall of judgment: and it was early; and they themselves went not into the judgment hall, lest they should be defiled; but <u>that they might eat the passover</u>." (John 18:28)

There was obviously a one-day difference in timing of Passover observance – "they" had not yet eaten of the Passover meal. Feast days were sometimes observed on different days by different groups due to:

Difficulty in determining the new moons
Sectarian differences in belief
Adjustments for convenience

> Our modern society also adjusts days around holidays to make
> long weekends for convenience or business purposes.

The Pharisees and other conservatives would have counted Thursday as Nisan 14 while the Sadducees, who dominated the priesthood, and other liberals and the Jewish leaders, would have reckoned Passover to be on Friday and would have eaten the Passover meal Friday evening. Most of the people would have recognized that Jesus' death came at the same time as the "official" slaying of the Passover Lamb in the temple. Yet Jesus observed Nisan 14 at the right time, a day earlier than the majority of the people.

This explains the difference between John 18:28 and what Matthew, Mark and Luke (referred to as the synoptic gospel writers) say about the time of Passover. They are giving the timing according to what Jesus and the Pharisees would have observed, and John is giving the time of the Sadducees' observance.

An important point to make here is that since Jesus and His disciples understood Nisan 14, (Passover) to be on Thursday and ate the Passover meal that evening, then it follows that the crucifixion happened the next day, Friday, Nisan 15. Many will object because they say that Jesus' death must match the day that for long centuries foreshadowed it. Since both positions have scriptural backing, we must look for a scriptural way to reconcile the two. The problem will be solved in Chapter Seven. This study will follow the position that Jesus' reckoning of the days was correct. Therefore, you will see some references to Nisan 14 being on Thursday.

References to the Preparation Day

The following passages, one from each of the synoptic gospels, when examined in context, show that preparation for the Passover meal as observed by Jesus and His disciples happened the day before the crucifixion:

> "Now the first *day* of the *feast of* unleavened bread the disciples came to Jesus, saying unto him, Where wilt thou that we prepare for thee <u>to eat the passover?</u>"
> (Matt 26:17)

"And the first day of unleavened bread, when they killed the passover, his disciples said unto him, Where wilt thou that we go and <u>prepare that thou mayest eat the passover</u>? And he sendeth forth <u>two of his disciples</u>, and saith unto them, Go ye into the city, and there shall meet you a man bearing a pitcher of water: follow him. And wheresoever he shall go in, say ye to the goodman of the house, The Master saith, Where is the guestchamber, <u>where I shall eat the passover</u> with my disciples?" (Mark 14:12-14)

"Then came the day of unleavened bread, <u>when the passover must be killed</u>. And <u>he sent</u> <u>Peter and John</u>, saying, Go and <u>prepare us the passover</u>, that we may eat. ... where I shall eat the passover with my disciples? ... and they made ready the passover." (Luke 22:7-8, 11, 13)

It is obvious from the verses above that the preparation referred to was that of Nisan 14, the day for killing and preparing the sacrifice and making ready the Passover meal. The disciples came to Jesus that day, Nisan 14, to ask about making preparations. He told Peter and John to go into the city, find and follow a certain man to the location and there make everything ready. Jesus' somewhat obscure directions (He didn't directly tell them a location) to only two of His disciples, may have been given to prevent Judas from knowing the exact location for the meal ahead of time. This may have been done by Jesus to prevent being interrupted during the Passover meal by an attempt to capture Him. The directions to the two disciples are recorded by Mark immediately after the verse which says: "he sought how he [Judas] might conveniently betray him." (Mark 14:11)

> The disciples did not make the preparations on Nisan 13. It was already the day "when the passover must be killed" when they first asked about it.

They made the preparations for the meal and then we are told:

"Now when the even was come, he sat down with the twelve." (Matt 26:20)

After partaking of the Passover meal, Jesus and the apostles went to the Garden of Gethsemane where they were met by Judas and the band of men sent to arrest Jesus. About the next day, the day of the crucifixion, John writes:

"Then led they Jesus from Caiaphas unto the hall of judgment: and it was early; and they themselves went not into the judgment hall, lest they should be defiled; but <u>that they might eat the passover</u>." (John 18:28)

"And <u>it was the preparation of the passover</u>, and about the sixth hour: and he saith unto the Jews, Behold your King!" (John 19:14)

John here refers to the day Jesus died as the Passover Day. As we have seen, the synoptic gospels record Passover as being the previous day. An important point to realize is that if John and the synoptics had a one-day difference in their recording of which day was Passover (Nisan 14), they would have to have the same one-day difference for the Feast of Unleavened Bread (Nisan 15).

Now, if we examine each of the following four verses (in their contexts), one from each of the four gospel writers including John, we will see that the preparation day referred to is always the day Jesus died:

> "Now the next day, that followed <u>the day of the preparation</u>, the chief priests and Pharisees came together unto Pilate," (Matt 27:62)

> "And now when the even was come, because it was <u>the preparation</u>, that is, <u>the day before the sabbath</u>," (Mark 15:42)

> "And that day [that Jesus was laid in the tomb] was <u>the preparation</u>, and the sabbath drew on." (Luke 23:54)

> "There laid they Jesus therefore because of <u>the Jews' preparation</u> *day*; for the sepulchre was nigh at hand." (John 19:42)

In each of these four verses, the word "preparation" is translated from the Greek "paraskeue" (*Strong's* NT#3904) which is never used in reference to anything other than the day before a seventh-day Sabbath. In each of the first three verses (Matthew 26:17, Mark 14:12 and Luke 22:8) we looked at in this section "prepare" was translated from the Greek word "hetoimazo" (*Strong's* NT#2090) which means to make ready or to prepare. The Greek word "paraskeue" was not used. Mark also designates the preparation day as "the day before the sabbath" with Sabbath being translated from the Greek word "prosabbaton" (*Strong's* NT #4315) which is a combination of "pro" (*Strong's* NT#4253) and "sabbaton" (*Strong's* NT#4521). As pointed out in the section later in this chapter "A Word Study on 'Sabbath' in the Old Testament," sabbaton is only used for a seventh-day Sabbath.

> Matthew, Mark and Luke are called the "synoptic" (seeing with the same eyes) gospels because of their similarities.

The synoptic gospel writers and John are in agreement that the crucifixion day was a day of preparation for a Sabbath to follow. This is strong evidence that the following day was a weekly seventh-day Sabbath and not a ceremonial Sabbath. The synoptic gospels refer to Nisan 14 and 15 as being on different days than John does, yet they refer to the preparation for the seventh-day Sabbath as being the same day. The synoptic gospels refer to the order of days as:

1. The day before the crucifixion "when the passover must be killed," (and therefore Nisan 14) and when the disciples prepared the Passover meal.

2. The day of the crucifixion, Nisan 15, the first day of the Feast of Unleavened Bread, an annual Sabbath and the day on which, in the early evening hours, Jesus ate the Passover with His disciples. It was also, as the verses above show, the preparation day for a seventh-day Sabbath.
3. The day after the crucifixion, Nisan 16, a seventh-day Sabbath.

John would be referring to the order of days as:

1. The day before the crucifixion, an ordinary day but the day on which the disciples prepared the Passover meal.
2. The day of the crucifixion, the Passover day (according to the Sadducees) and a day of preparation for a seventh-day Sabbath.
3. The day after the crucifixion, a seventh-day Sabbath and the first day of the Feast of Unleavened Bread (according to the Sadducees).

Whatever differences they might have had in recording the feast days, the gospel writers would be in agreement as to which day was the seventh-day Sabbath. Since they reported differently which day was Passover (Nisan 14) but all agreed that the crucifixion day was a day of preparation for a Sabbath, the following day must have been a seventh-day Sabbath. The relation of the days and the verses referring to them can be better understood by referring to the following diagram that compares the reckoning of days by the synoptic gospel writers and by John:

Day:	Thursday		Friday		Saturday	
	Nisan 14		Nisan 15		Nisan 16	
Reckoning of days by the Pharisees and Jesus; reported in synoptic gospels:						
Disciples prepare Passover		Day of the Crucifixion		Day of the Resurrection		
Matt 26:17-19 Mark 14:12-16 Luke 22:7-13	All refer to preparation day for the Passover meal	Matt 27:62 Mark 15:42 Luke 23:54, 56 John 19:31	All refer to preparation for a 7th-day Sabbath	Matt 28:1 Mark 16:1 Luke 24:1	Correctly understood as a 7th-day Sabbath	
Passover day		Feast of Unleavened Bread		Feast of First Fruits		
Reckoning of days by the Sadducees and chief priests; reported by John:						
		Passover day		Feast of Unleavened Bread		
		John 19:14	Preparation of the Passover	John 20:1	Correctly understood as a 7th-day Sabbath	

The Wednesday Crucifixion Theory

The Wednesday crucifixion theory which is popular with some people, is used to allow for Jesus being three days and three nights in the grave, actually, exactly 72 hours. Its adherents then, in most cases, place the resurrection on Sabbath (Saturday) afternoon.

The Wednesday Crucifixion advocates maintain an order of days as:

> Nisan 14, Wednesday - the crucifixion
> Nisan 15, Thursday - the first day of the Feast of Unleavened Bread, a Sabbath
> Nisan 16, Friday - not a holy day but the weekly day of preparation for the seventh-day Sabbath and the day the women would have purchased the spices
> Nisan 17, Saturday – the weekly Sabbath and the day of the resurrection

The Wednesday theory would say that those verses that mention "preparation" on the crucifixion day, were all referring to Wednesday as the preparation day for the Thursday ceremonial Sabbath marking the first day of the Feast of Unleavened Bread. However, the reasoning above shows that this cannot be because John and the synoptic writers refer to Passover being on different days. The Passover day (Nisan 14) is the day of preparation for the Feast of Unleavened Bread.

There are other problems with the theory. It places the cleansing of the temple on a Sabbath, when there would have been no selling in the temple. The middle of the seven-day week, when they claim the crucifixion must have occurred, is actually about 6 am on a Wednesday morning, not 3 pm. The theory misses on this point by nine hours. Also, it extends Jesus time in the grave into a fourth day. See the section "When did the Women Come to the Tomb" in Chapter Five for an additional reason.

Most importantly, the Wednesday theory completely ignores the scriptural meaning of such terms as "heart" and "earth." In this study, we are seeing that there is a better, more-scriptural way to understand the "three days and three nights in the heart of the earth." With a correct understanding of "the first day of the week" and the above reasoning, everything works out for a Friday afternoon crucifixion time.

> Wednesday crucifixion advocates place Jesus' death in "the midst of the week" (Dan 9:27) but they miss that mark by nine hours.

The Feast of Unleavened Bread

The Feast of Unleavened Bread following directly after Passover was a seven-day feast during which they would eat no bread that contained leaven. Leaven was symbolic of sin and the feast helped to impress upon the people the need to remove sin from their lives. The Feast of Unleavened Bread was always, as specified in Lev 23:6, to begin on Nisan 15. As seen above, there were sectarian differences as to which day this fell on, either the Thursday or Friday of the week in that year. The Passover meal was eaten with unleavened bread on the first day of the feast:

> "And they shall eat the flesh in that night, roast with fire, and unleavened bread; *and* with bitter *herbs* they shall eat it." (Exo 12:8)

This makes sense as the meal was actually eaten in the evening hours of the first day of the Feast of Unleavened Bread. The first and last days of the feast are described as "holy convocations."

"And on the fifteenth day of the same month *is* the feast of unleavened bread unto the LORD: seven days ye must eat unleavened bread. In the first day ye shall have an <u>holy convocation</u>: ye shall do no servile work therein. But ye shall offer an offering made by fire unto the LORD seven days: in the seventh day *is* an <u>holy convocation</u>: ye shall do no servile work therein." (Lev 23:6-8)

The people were told to "have an holy convocation" and to "do no servile work" on the first and last days of the feast. In this way, they are like seventh-day Sabbaths and people sometimes refer to them as Sabbaths, but the Bible never calls them that. This becomes important in connection with the timing of the following spring feasts so we need to examine it carefully.

A Word Study on "Sabbath" in the Old Testament

The timing for the wave sheaf (First Fruits) and Pentecost is given as:

"And he shall wave the sheaf before the LORD, to be accepted for you: on the morrow after the <u>sabbath</u> the priest shall wave it." (Lev 23:11)

"And ye shall count unto you from the morrow after the <u>sabbath</u>, from the day that ye brought the sheaf of the wave offering; seven sabbaths shall be complete: Even unto the morrow after the seventh sabbath shall ye number fifty days; and ye shall offer a new meat offering unto the LORD." (Lev 23:15-16)

The big question is: "what Sabbath is being referred to?" Many people maintain that "the sabbath" is referring to the first day of the Feast of Unleavened Bread (Nisan 15) which, they say, is a Sabbath. By this reckoning, the Feast of First Fruits and Pentecost can fall on any day of the week. So we need to determine if the word "sabbath" as used in these verses could be referring to the first day of the Feast of Unleavened Bread, or whether it only means the seventh-day Sabbath.

The two Hebrew words commonly translated as "Sabbath" in the Old Testament are "Shabbath" (*Strong's* OT#7676) and "Shabbathon" (*Strong's* OT#7677).

"Shabbath" is always used to refer to a seventh-day Sabbath, or, in a few cases, the seventh year, or the Day of Atonement, occurring in the seventh month. Feast days other than the Day of Atonement are never referred to using this word. There are two verses where, in the King James Bible, the word "sabbath" occurs three times in connection with a feast day:

"Speak unto the children of Israel, saying, In the seventh month, in the first *day* of the month, shall ye have a <u>sabbath</u>, a memorial of blowing of trumpets, an holy convocation." (Lev 23:24)

"Also in the fifteenth day of the seventh month, when ye have gathered in the fruit of the land, ye shall keep a feast unto the LORD seven days: on the first day *shall be* a <u>sabbath</u>, and on the eighth day *shall be* a <u>sabbath</u>." (Lev 23:39)

> Original words are not always translated consistently. Often it helps to examine how words are used, to discern possible mistranslations.

However, if you check in a concordance, you will see that the original word used in these verses is "Shabbathon." Every other time this word is used in the original, the King James Version translates it as "rest." The two words are often used together as in:

> "Six days may work be done; but in the seventh *is* the <u>sabbath</u> (Shabbath) of <u>rest</u> (Shabbathon), holy to the LORD ..." (Exo 31:15)

Clearly, they do not mean the same thing and are not interchangeable. Thus, in Leviticus 23:11, 15-16 "sabbath" which is translated from "shabbath" is clearly referring to the seventh-day Sabbath, and not the first day of the Feast of Unleavened Bread. We will find yet more evidence later. This makes determination of the Feast of First Fruits easier. Correctly understanding the original words translated as "sabbath," shows that its timing is determined in relation to the seventh-day Sabbath.

The Feast of First Fruits

Moses was told:

> "Speak unto the children of Israel, and say unto them, When ye be come into the land which I give unto you, and shall reap the harvest thereof, then ye shall bring a sheaf of the firstfruits of your harvest unto the priest: And he shall wave the sheaf before the LORD, to be accepted for you: on the morrow after the sabbath the priest shall wave it." (Lev 23:10-11)

This offering was "to be accepted "<u>for you</u>" or "so it will be accepted <u>on your behalf</u>" (*New International Version*), or "<u>for your acceptance</u>" (*KJ3 Literal Translation*). This was not an offering so that the Messiah would be accepted, but rather that we (physical Israel then, spiritual Israel now) would be accepted. The grain offered at the feast represents the Messiah, but was being elevated so that His followers would be accepted.

> As angels gather the final harvest, will groups (sheaves) of waiting people be waving their arms to attract their attention?

The procedure at this feast is described thus:

"The Mishnah, written a few centuries after the time of the first century church, describes how a messenger would go out and bind the standing stalks of grain into sheaves so that it would be easy to cut. The priest, followed by his entourage, would come to the field, sickle in hand, and ask, 'Is the sun set?' to which the people would answer, 'Yes!!' 'Shall I reap?' 'Reap!!' The priest then cut off a standing stalk of grain, then took it to be prepared for the offering the next morning.

The wave sheaf had been chosen in advance, as Christ was. It was tied in a bundle, symbolizing His captivity. It was cut loose from the ground just at sunset – just the time at which Christ rose from the dead after three days and three nights in the tomb. The cutting of the grain symbolized Christ's actual resurrection."
(Jack M. Lane, *The Wave Sheaf Offering -- The Forgotten Holy Day?*)

Of course, the reference in this quote to Christ rising "after three days and three nights in the tomb" is not in agreement with this study but the quotation is helpful in understanding the wave sheaf procedure. The morning after it was cut it was taken to the temple.

"When they arrived at the Temple, the priest would take the sheaves, lift some in the air and wave them in every direction to acknowledge God's sovereignty over the whole earth. Before the offering of the sheaves, no reaping of the harvest for personal use could be done (Lev 23:14)." (Samuel Bacchiocchi, *God's Festivals in Scripture and History Part 1: The Spring Festivals*, p. 171)

The important thing about the wave sheaf was not that it was cut or cut off (as in death) but that it was harvested (as in resurrection). The ultimate harvest is the end of the world when the ripe fruit (Christians with fully-matured, Christ-like characters) will be harvested:

"For the Lord himself shall descend from heaven with a shout, with the voice of the archangel, and with the trump of God: and the dead in Christ shall rise first: Then we which are alive *and* remain shall be caught up together with them in the clouds, to meet the Lord in the air: and so shall we ever be with the Lord."
(1 Thess 4:16-17)

Jesus was "harvested" at His resurrection on the Sabbath, likely just after sunset in accordance with the types of the Feast of First Fruits, and returned to heaven the next morning with those that were raised with Him as the first fruits, to be waved or presented before the Father. This is a further clue that His actual resurrection may have happened at, or just after sunset. Those that were raised with Him also were "harvested" on the Feast of First Fruits by their resurrection; they were obviously not harvested by being killed. Their death had happened previously; for some of them perhaps years earlier.

> Harvest terminology is frequent in the Bible. For example: "… Thrust in thy sickle, and reap: … for the harvest of the earth is ripe." (Rev 14:15)

A Word Study of "After"

There is one more translation issue that needs to be solved to properly understand the timing of the wave-sheaf offering. That involves the use of the word "after" in these verses:

> "And he shall wave the sheaf before the LORD, to be accepted, for you: on the morrow <u>after</u> the sabbath the priest shall wave it:" (Lev 23:11)

> "And ye shall count unto you from the morrow <u>after</u> the sabbath, from the day that ye brought the sheaf of the wave offering; seven sabbaths shall be complete."
> (Lev 23:15)

> "Even unto the morrow <u>after</u> the seventh sabbath shall ye number fifty days; and ye shall offer a new meat offering unto the LORD." (Lev 23:16)

We have already seen that the word "sabbath" can only mean the seventh-day Sabbath. These verses would then seem to indicate that the wave sheaf and Pentecost must always be on Sundays in every year. This conflicts with the findings of this book that Jesus was resurrected and presented as the wave sheaf offering on a seventh-day Sabbath. How can this be resolved?

As we have already done with several words and phrases in this study, we need to carefully examine the original words. The first clue is found by examining *Strong's Concordance* which indicates that, in each of these verses, "morrow" is translated from the Hebrew word "mochorath" (*Strong's* OT#4283) and "the sabbath" is translated from the Hebrew "shabbath" (*Strong's* OT#7676) but there is no word in the original Hebrew verse which could be translated into the word "after."

The original word "shabbath" is never translated "after the sabbath" in the King James Version except in these verses. There is a Hebrew word "achar" (*Strong's* OT#310) that is translated as "after" in 454 cases of its use and in one verse clearly means and is used in the phrase "after the sabbath:"

> "And it came to pass, that when the gates of Jerusalem began to be dark before the sabbath, I commanded that the gates should be shut, and charged that they should not be opened till <u>after the sabbath</u>: and *some* of my servants set I at the gates, *that* there should no burden be brought in on the sabbath day." (Neh 13:19)

This arbitrary addition of the word "after" in Leviticus 23, verses 11, 15 and 16 obviously changes the meaning as it is not in the original, and is not consistent with any of the other 100 plus translations of "shabbath." The Hebrew word "mochorath" does not mean or include the meaning of "after."

A more correct translation than "on the morrow after the sabbath" would be "the morrow of the sabbath," or "the following sabbath," or "the next sabbath." In the case of Lev 23:16, it would be "the morrow of the seventh sabbath." Here are some more literal translations:

> "then he hath waved the sheaf before Jehovah for your acceptance; <u>on the morrow of the sabbath</u> doth the priest wave it." (Lev 23:11, *Young's Literal Translation*)

> "then he shall wave the sheaf before Jehovah for your acceptance; <u>on the morrow of the sabbath</u> the priest shall wave it." (Lev 23:11, *KJ3 Literal Translation*)

> "And ye have numbered to you <u>from the morrow of the sabbath</u>, from the day of your bringing in the sheaf of the wave-offering: they are seven perfect sabbaths;" (Lev 23:15, *Young's Literal Translation*)

> "unto <u>the morrow of the seventh sabbath</u> ye do number fifty days, and ye have brought near a new present to Jehovah;" (Lev 23:16, *Young's Literal Translation*)

With this understanding, we can see that the First Fruits were offered (waved) on the morrow <u>of</u> the seventh-day Sabbath not on the morrow <u>after</u> the Sabbath. This is consistent with our understanding of Jesus' resurrection. He was presented as the wave sheaf offering on Sabbath morning, after His resurrection earlier on Sabbath evening – what we would call Friday evening. This is consistent with how the Feast of First Fruits was observed.

An important note here is that, as Jesus is our example in all things, we can use the timing of the events in His life to check what is reported to have happened elsewhere in scripture. Not that the word of God is wrong but, as we have seen, there are a few translation issues that have had a serious effect on our understanding.

The Passover as Israel Left Egypt

It is interesting to look at the original Passover, when Israel left their captivity in Egypt. Since Joseph was a type of Christ and he was, in a sense, resurrected when his bones were taken from their burial place in Succoth, is it possible that that event happened on the Feast of First Fruits? This was in fulfillment of the promise Joseph had required of Israel before his death:

> "And Moses took the bones of Joseph with him: for he had straitly sworn the children of Israel, saying, God will surely visit you; and ye shall carry up my bones away hence with you." (Exo 13:19)

Succoth was the first camping place of the Israelites as they were fleeing from Egypt. The days can be compared to the days of crucifixion week like this:

	Sunday	Monday	Tuesday	Wednesday	Thursday	Friday	Saturday
	Nisan 10	Nisan 11	Nisan 12	Nisan 13	Nisan 14	Nisan 15	Nisan 16
Jesus	Triumphal entry				Passover	FUB	FFF – Jesus raised
Egypt	Exo 12:3 "in the tenth *day* … take … a lamb"				Passover	FUB – left Egypt Exo 12:17 Gen 50:25 Num 33:3	Succoth – Joseph "raised" Exo 13:19 Num 33:5

FUB = Feast of Unleavened Bread; FFF = Feast of First Fruits

Jesus was resurrected from the tomb of Joseph of Ramah (Arimathaea in Greek). "Ramah … means 'seat of idolatry' in Hebrew." (Joseph Good, *Rosh HaShanah and the Messianic Kingdom to Come.* p. 24). This city is identified with the present location of Ramallah about nine miles north of Jerusalem. Just as Jesus' resurrection from the tomb of Joseph of Arimathea assures us that we are going to the Promised Land, the removal of the bones of Joseph, who lived in Rameses in Egypt, the seat of idolatry, from his tomb, indicated to Pharaoh that Israel was headed to the Promised Land and not returning to Egypt. That may be why he pursued after them.

Pentecost

Pentecost was the day Israel gave thanks for the spring wheat harvest. The name is derived from the Greek word "pentekoste" meaning "fiftieth." It was also called the Feast of Weeks, implying not just 50 days but a number of weeks:

> "And thou shalt observe the feast of weeks, of the firstfruits of wheat harvest …"
> (Exo 34:22)

> The Jews counted seven complete weeks, and including the Sabbath they
> started from, 50 complete days from First Fruits to Pentecost.

They were told when to start counting the weeks:

> "Seven weeks shalt thou number unto thee: begin to number the seven weeks from *such time as* thou beginnest *to put* the sickle to the corn." (Deut 16:9)

The first sheaf was cut just after the start of the seventh-day Sabbath that marked the Feast of First Fruits. So they would start counting weeks on that day and count seven full weeks which would bring them to the fiftieth day, another seventh-day Sabbath and the Feast of Pentecost. This would result in a count of seven full seven-day weeks, and not parts of a week at the beginning and ending of the fifty days, which would happen if the count started midweek.

They were also told to count Sabbaths:

"And ye shall count unto you from the morrow after the sabbath, from the day that ye brought the sheaf of the wave offering; <u>seven sabbaths shall be complete:</u>" (Lev 23:15)

The following verse gives evidence of this counting process:

"And it came to pass on the second sabbath after the first, that he went through the corn fields; and his disciples plucked the ears of corn, and did eat, rubbing *them* in *their* hands." (Luke 6:1)

What is "the second sabbath after the first?" This is explained in Johnston Cheney's discussion of this verse:

"Seven sabbaths were to be counted from the Feast of First-fruits or Passover. Consequently, these came to be known as 'First Sabbath,' 'Second Sabbath' etc., down to the seventh. And according to Julian Morgenstern, former President of Hebrew University, this practice continued in Galilee till the time of Christ or the Common Era. It is still observed by some groups in Palestine today. Thus, there was an annual date known as 'First Sabbath,' just after Passover." (Johnston Cheney, *The Life of Christ in Stereo: The Four Gospels Speak in Harmony*, p. 230)

Again, this is logical considering that they were told to count Sabbaths.

The first day of the Feast of Unleavened Bread, Nisan 15, is linked unquestionably to Passover, Nisan 14, as the following day. Just as certainly, Pentecost is linked to the Feast of First Fruits being the 50th day from (and including) the day of that feast. Thus, whatever day of the week the Feast of First Fruits occurs on, Pentecost would be on the same day of the week. We have established above, that the Feast of First Fruits is always on the seventh-day Sabbath falling within the Feast of Unleavened Bread.

In the following diagram, the Feast of First Fruits (FFF), which is also the first of the 50 days leading up to Pentecost, could shift back and forth from year to year and land on any of the seven days of the Feast of Unleavened Bread (FUB), whichever one of those was the seventh-day Sabbath.

	Day 1 FFF 7th-day Sabbath	Day 2	Day 3	Day 4	Day 5	~	Day 49	Day 50 Pent. 7th-day Sabbath
	← the 7th-day Sabbath would be on a different day each year →							
Pass-over	FUB day 1	FUB day 2	FUB day 3	FUB Day 4	FUB day 5	FUB day 6	FUB day 7	
Nisan 14	Nisan 15	Nisan 16	Nisan 17	Nisan 18	Nisan 19	Nisan 20	Nisan 21	

FFF = Feast of First Fruits; Pent. = Pentecost; FUB = Feast of Unleavened Bread

Counting fifty days inclusive from the Feast of First Fruits brings us to the Feast of Pentecost, which would be on another seventh-day Sabbath. Now everything in the timing fits according to scripture. There are fifty days inclusive from the Feast of First Fruits to Pentecost and there are seven complete weeks with the last week ending on a seventh-day Sabbath.

Let's consider what would happen to the determination of the timing of Pentecost if Feast Days were considered to be Sabbaths. The seventh day of the Feast of Unleavened Bread would have to be counted and Pentecost itself would be included even if not on a seventh-day Sabbath. There could easily be nine Sabbaths in the 50-day period. See *Appendix 4 - Possible Counts of Days from Feast of First Fruits to Pentecost*, p. 126.

There is another problem with the common theory of the Feasts of First Fruits and Pentecost being on fixed days of the month, rather than fixed days of the week. Pentecost is described as being:

> "Even unto <u>the morrow after the seventh sabbath</u> shall ye number fifty days; and
> ye shall offer a new meat offering unto the LORD." (Lev 23:16)

If Pentecost, 50 days inclusive from the Feast of First Fruits, ends up being midweek what Sabbath is it following? There is none specified. The 49th day of the count is not designated as a Sabbath. With the word "after" removed it all makes sense.

We now have considerable evidence for a correct understanding of the order and timing of the major events. (Refer again to the diagram in the section "The End of the Three Days and Three Nights" near the end of Chapter Two.) The "three days and three nights" was a literal time period. It began on Tuesday evening, with the betrayal by Judas to the chief priests and ended with Jesus death on Friday afternoon, Nisan 15. The Passover day for slaying the lambs was on Thursday, Nisan 14; the Passover meal was eaten by Jesus and His disciples on Thursday evening followed by the handover, and then Jesus' trials and crucifixion on Friday. He was buried just before sunset and rose shortly after. He ascended (briefly) to heaven on the Feast of First Fruits on Sabbath morning. Fifty days later, also on a seventh-day Sabbath, was Pentecost. In the next chapter, we will go back to a few days before the crucifixion and follow in detail the order of events through to the resurrection. It should all fit together in a logical and scripturally-consistent manner.

Chapter 5 – The Chronology of Events of Jesus' Last Week

The Lamb Kept in the Home

The Jews were instructed to do something else at Passover season that was meant to give them a better understanding of the character of God. At the time of the Exodus they were commanded:

> " … In the tenth *day* of this month they shall take to them every man a lamb, according to the house of *their* fathers, a lamb for an house:" (Exo 12:3)

Each household was to select a lamb and then verse 6 says:

> "And ye shall keep it up until the fourteenth day of the same month: and the whole assembly of the congregation of Israel shall kill it in the evening." (Exo 12:6)

So, from the tenth to the fourteenth day they were to have this lamb "without blemish, a male of the first year," (verse 5) in their home. They would get to know it almost like a pet and appreciate its character. In Jesus' time, they would have been familiar with the passage:

> "He was oppressed, and he was afflicted, yet he opened not his mouth: he is brought as a lamb to the slaughter, and as a sheep before her shearers is dumb, so he openeth not his mouth." (Isa 53:7)

> Can you imagine keeping a little lamb in or close by your house as a pet for this length of time? You could become quite attached to it.

The whole reason for taking a lamb was to help them recognize the real Lamb of God whom John the Baptist introduced later:

> "… John seeth Jesus coming unto him, and saith, Behold the Lamb of God, which taketh away the sin of the world." (John 1:29)

Jesus is described in later scriptures in terms consistent with the lamb and its character:

> "But with the precious blood of Christ, as of a lamb without blemish and without spot:" (1 Pet 1:19)

> "For such an high priest became us, *who is* holy, harmless, undefiled, separate from sinners, and made higher than the heavens;" (Heb 7:26)

Doesn't "harmless" and "undefiled" describe a lamb of the first year? Now let's consider when the tenth of Nisan occurred in the year of the crucifixion.

> "Then Jesus six days before the passover came to Bethany, where Lazarus was which had been dead, whom he raised from the dead. ... On the next day [Sunday] much people that were come to the feast, when they heard that Jesus was coming to Jerusalem, Took branches of palm trees, and went forth to meet him, and cried, Hosanna: Blessed *is* the King of Israel that cometh in the name of the Lord." (John 12:1, 12-13)

We saw in Chapter Four, that John referred to Passover being on Friday which was actually Nisan 15 by Jesus' reckoning. Six days previous would be the previous Sabbath, on Nisan 9. "On the next day" would be referring to Sunday, Nisan 10. That Sunday was the day, commonly referred to as Palm Sunday, when Jesus made His entry into Jerusalem from Bethany.

Here is a diagram of the relationship of the Triumphal Entry into Jerusalem on Sunday to the other days of the week:

Sunday	Monday	Tuesday	Wednesday	Thursday	Friday	Saturday
Nisan 10	Nisan 11	Nisan 12	Nisan 13	Nisan 14/ Pass	Nisan 15/ FUB	Nisan 16/ FFF
First Day	Second day	Third Day	Fourth Day	Fifth Day	Preparation	Sabbath
E					S P	D R

Pass. = Passover; FUB = Feast of Unleavened Bread; FFF = Feast of First Fruits;
E = Entry into Jerusalem; S = Sacrifice of lambs for Thursday Passover observance;
P = Passover meal (Jesus' observance); D = Death; R = Resurrection

Nisan 10 happened to be on a Sunday that year but it would fall on a Sunday only one year in seven. There is nothing here to support Sunday sacredness; certainly scripture does not make it a holy day. Scripture specifies that the selection of the lamb be on Nisan 10, which again could be on any day of the week. The record of events from this point to the crucifixion will also support that the lamb selection, and Jesus' entry into Jerusalem, were on a Sunday. Remember, as discussed in Chapter Four, by Jesus' reckoning, Nisan 14 was on Thursday so the crucifixion was then on Friday, Nisan 15. Again, this seeming discrepancy will be discussed in Chapter Seven.

The actual lamb used in the official Passover ceremony was selected in Bethany and taken by the priests in a procession to Jerusalem, through the Sheep Gate and into the temple. Crowds of people ("a very great multitude," Matt 21:8) gathered to watch this official ceremony and the people in the procession would chant Psalm 118. See, for example, verse 26:

> "Blessed *be* he that cometh in the name of the LORD ..." (Psa 118:26)

As this official ceremony was in process:

> "… Jesus, when he had found a young ass, sat thereon; as it is written, Fear not,
> daughter of Sion: behold, thy King cometh, sitting on an ass's colt."
> (John 12:14-15)

**Jesus joined the parade traveling from Bethany to Jerusalem,
but He soon became the major attraction.**

Jesus joined the procession as the Passover lamb was taken from Bethany to Jerusalem, through the Sheep Gate and into the temple. He was coming to Jerusalem as the True Lamb of God to which all the sacrificial lambs over the centuries had pointed, and following the route they took. The timing was perfect. It was a fulfillment of prophecy, and many people would have later understood it as one more piece of evidence pointing to Jesus as the Messiah. Certainly His disciples did:

> "These things understood not his disciples at the first; but when Jesus was glorified,
> then remembered they that these things were written of him, and *that* they had
> done these things unto him." (John 12:16)

They would have recalled the prophecy:

> "Rejoice greatly, O daughter of Zion; shout, O daughter of Jerusalem: behold, thy
> King cometh unto thee: he *is* just, and having salvation; lowly, and riding upon
> an ass, and upon a colt the foal of an ass." (Zech 9:9)

After arriving in Jerusalem, Jesus visited the temple:

> "And Jesus entered into Jerusalem, and into the temple: and when he had looked
> round about upon all things, and now the eventide was come, he went out unto
> Bethany with the twelve." (Mark 11:11)

From Sunday (Nisan 10) to Thursday (Nisan 14), Jesus, the true Passover Lamb, spent the time (as specified in Exodus) in Jerusalem and especially in the temple being examined by the leaders and the people to give them opportunity to judge if He qualified as the "sacrificial lamb." They of course, were not thinking of that but many certainly were examining Him carefully to find any fault. He would retire each night, as mentioned in the verse above, to Bethany where His friends Lazarus, Mary and Martha lived, and where He was further from His enemies in Jerusalem. Later, when He was examined by Pilate, the governor of Jerusalem, Pilate declared his opinion of Jesus:

> "Then said Pilate to the chief priests and *to* the people, I find no fault in this man."
> (Luke 23:4)

> Never was a sacrificial "lamb" inspected more carefully; never was a sacrificial lamb found that was more perfect.

Summary of Events During the Days of Examination

A careful comparison between the gospels, and some sound reasoning, helps determine the order and timing of events. The Gospel of Mark seems to be the one that reports events in the most chronological order as follows:

Monday Morning
>Returned from Bethany (Mark 11:12)
>The barren fig tree cursed (Mark 11:13-14)
>The temple cleansed (Mark 11:15-16)

Monday Evening
>Left Jerusalem (Mark 11:19)

Tuesday Morning
>Saw the fig tree withered (Mark 11:20)
>Arrived again in Jerusalem (Mark 11:27-28)
>Questioned (examined) by the chief priests, scribes and elders (Mark 11:27)
>Spoke in parables (Mark 12:1)
>Questioned (examined) by the Pharisees and Herodians (Mark 12:13)
>Questioned (examined) by the Sadducees (Mark 12:18)
>Questioned (examined) by one of the scribes (Mark 12:28)
>No one dared ask Him any more questions (Mark 12:34)
>>(They could find no fault in the Lamb)
>He continued teaching in the temple (Mark 12:35)
>The common people heard Him gladly (Mark 12:37)
>He went out of the temple (Mark 13:1)
>Olivet discourse (Matthew 24, Mark 13, Luke 21)
>Two days until Passover (Mark 14:1)
>>(Note: Jesus observed Passover on Thursday)
>Despite finding no fault, the Lamb is rejected and the chief priests
>>and scribes conspire to bring about His death (Mark 14:1)

Tuesday Evening
>Dinner at Simon the leper's house in Bethany (Mark 14:3)
>>(Details on timing of dinner below)
>Judas leaves the dinner to betray Him (Mark 14:10)

Thursday Morning
>The disciples asked where to prepare the Passover meal (Mark 14:12)

Thursday Evening
>Jesus ate the Passover meal with the twelve (Mark 14:17-18)

The events of Tuesday, all the questioning by different groups and the teaching in the temple, would have taken some time. Then there is the Olivet discourse and, early in chapter 14 Mark mentions the plotting of His death by His enemies. By then it could easily be approaching Tuesday evening. The next event mentioned is the dinner at Simon's house, from which Judas left to betray Jesus to those who had murder in their hearts. Their decision had been made that He had to die. This point (Tuesday evening, following the supper) coincides with the beginning of the three days and three nights. We know this because Jesus always started the series of events that made up the three days and three nights, with His betrayal as discussed in Chapter Two.

Timing of the Supper at Simon's House

You will notice that as John 12:2-11 describes Jesus' attendance at a supper in Bethany, the timing seems to be different than in the other gospels (Matthew 26 and Mark 14) where the supper is described as being two days before Passover (Matt 26:2, Mark 14:1) and following Palm Sunday (as outlined above). It is the same event; John, while starting his narrative by saying, "Then Jesus six days before the passover came to Bethany …" (John 12:1), just inserts the story of the supper (verses 2-11) parenthetically at this point. He makes the connection by the word "there" at the start of verse 2. He is describing what happened "there" – there in Bethany; He is not describing events in order. John does the same thing in other places in his writings, for example, in Revelation 20, where He is talking about the first and second resurrections of the dead:

> "… and they lived and reigned with Christ a thousand years. (But the rest of the dead lived not again until the thousand years were finished.) This *is* the first resurrection. Blessed and holy *is* he that hath part in the first resurrection: on such the second death hath no power, but they shall be priests of God and of Christ, and shall reign with him a thousand years." (Rev 20:4-6)

I added the parentheses in the passage above but it obviously is a parenthetical statement. His topic is the first resurrection which happens at the start of the thousand years. He adds the sentence about the rest of the dead, who are raised in the second resurrection at the end of the thousand years, to explain when they are raised, then returns to his topic of the first resurrection.

Also, remember, that John uses the other method of reckoning for Passover. When he says, "Then Jesus six days before the Passover came to Bethany" (John 12:1), since he reckons Passover as Friday, he is referring to the previous Saturday. We understand that Jesus ate the Passover meal on Thursday evening, which would make Thursday (Wednesday sunset to Thursday sunset) the 14th of Nisan. Then back up to the 10th of Nisan and we'll come to Sunday.

Timing of the Crucifixion and Death

Mark records the time of the crucifixion:

> "And it was the third hour, and they crucified him." (Mark 15:25)

> Bible historian Joseph Good says that the Passover Lamb was
> bound to the altar in the temple at about 9 am.

However, John seems to be recording an earlier event, Jesus' appearance before Pilate, as happening later:

> "And it was the preparation of the passover, and about the sixth hour: and he [Pilate] saith unto the Jews, Behold your King!" (John 19:14)

This apparent discrepancy is resolved by understanding that the Romans counted the hours differently than the Jews. John, in this instance, is reporting the hour according to Roman time which he may have done because the event actually happened on Roman territory, in Pilate's court. In the Roman system each day was divided into 24 hours reckoned to begin, as with us, at midnight. Thus John says that Jesus was before Pilate at the sixth hour, or as we would say, about 6 am.

Mark writes that Jesus was crucified at the third hour, according to the Jewish system which is counting hours from sunrise. By that system, the third hour, three hours after sunrise, would be 9 am. The synoptic gospel writers also said that there was darkness from the sixth hour until the ninth hour (Matt 27:45, Mark 15:33, and Luke 23:44) and that Jesus died at the ninth hour (Matt 27:46, Mark 15:34):

> "And about the ninth hour Jesus cried with a loud voice, saying, Eli, Eli, lama sabachthani? that is to say, My God, my God, why hast thou forsaken me? Some of them that stood there, when they heard *that*, said, This *man* calleth for Elias. And straightway one of them ran, and took a spunge, and filled *it* with vinegar, and put *it* on a reed, and gave him to drink. The rest said, Let be, let us see whether Elias will come to save him. Jesus, when he had cried again with a loud voice, yielded up the ghost." (Matt 27:46-50)

At the time of His death there were some dramatic events:

> "And, behold, the veil of the temple was rent in twain from the top to the bottom; and the earth did quake, and the rocks rent; And the graves were opened; and many bodies of the saints which slept arose," (Matt 27:51-52)

For some thoughts on how the resurrection of the saints fits into the timing see *Appendix 5 – The Graves of the Saints Were Opened*, p. 128.

> Were people able to look into open tombs with human remains
> in them, from Friday evening until Sunday morning?

Thus, Jesus was on the cross for six hours, from 9 am when the sacrifice was normally bound to the altar, until 3 pm, the time of the evening sacrifice. It was perhaps another hour before His body was removed for a total of seven hours on the cross.

Events From Jesus' Death to Resurrection

Let's now trace the order of events from Jesus' death to His resurrection and try to determine just how short a time He might have actually been in the grave, and when He likely rose. This will also help us to understand the timing in the Gospel accounts.

1. The Jews Went to Pilate

The Jews were concerned about the requirement in Deuteronomy:

> "And if a man have committed a sin worthy of death, and he be to be put to death, and thou hang him on a tree: His body shall not remain all night upon the tree, but thou shalt in any wise bury him that day; (for he that is hanged is accursed of God;) that thy land be not defiled, which the LORD thy God giveth thee *for* an inheritance." (Deut 21:22-23)

Because of this, immediately after Jesus' death (John 19:30), they went to Pilate to request that the bodies be removed:

> "The Jews therefore, because it was the preparation, that the bodies should not remain upon the cross on the sabbath day, (for that sabbath day was an high day,) besought Pilate that their legs might be broken, and *that* they might be taken away." (John 19:31)

Once Pilate gave this order someone had to return to Golgotha with the order for the soldiers to carry out.

2. The Thieves' Legs Broken, Jesus' Side Pierced

> "Then came the soldiers, and brake the legs of the first, and of the other which was crucified with him. But when they came to Jesus, and saw that he was dead already, they brake not his legs: But one of the soldiers with a spear pierced his side, and forthwith came there out blood and water." (John 19:32-34)

> Breaking the legs was done to hasten death. In Jesus' case, this was not necessary. It was also a fulfillment of prophecy.

The centurion, having acknowledged that; "Truly this was the son of God" (Matt 27:54), would likely not have allowed the breaking of Jesus' legs out of respect for Him.

3. Joseph Went to Pilate

Then it says that "after this," after all these events:

> "And after this Joseph of Arimathaea, being a disciple of Jesus, but secretly for fear of the Jews, besought Pilate that he might take away the body of Jesus: and Pilate gave *him* leave. He came therefore, and took the body of Jesus." (John 19:38)

4. Pilate Called the Centurion

Mark adds that after Joseph made his request, Pilate called for the centurion to check if Jesus was really dead:

> "Joseph of Arimathaea, an honourable counsellor, which also waited for the kingdom of God, came, and went in boldly unto Pilate, and craved the body of Jesus. And Pilate marvelled if he were already dead: and <u>calling *unto him* the centurion</u>, he asked him whether he had been any while dead. And when he knew *it* of the centurion, he gave the body to Joseph." (Mark 15:43-45)

5. Jesus Removed From the Cross and Buried

> "And there came also Nicodemus, which at the first came to Jesus by night, and brought a mixture of myrrh and aloes, about an hundred pound *weight*. <u>Then took they [Joseph and Nicodemus] the body of Jesus</u>, and <u>wound it in linen clothes with the spices</u>, as the manner of the Jews is to bury. Now in the place where he was crucified there was a garden; and in the garden a new sepulchre, wherein was never man yet laid. There laid they Jesus therefore because of the Jews' preparation *day*; for the sepulchre was nigh at hand." (John 19:39-42)

> It was a good thing Joseph's tomb was available and nearby because the Sabbath was drawing close.

6. The Tomb Closed

> "And he [Joseph] bought fine linen, and took him down, and wrapped him in the linen, and laid him in a sepulchre which was hewn out of a rock, and rolled a stone unto the door of the sepulchre." (Mark 15:46)

Jesus had died, been removed from the cross and was in the tomb. Then Luke adds:

> "And that day was the preparation [Friday], and the sabbath drew on [it was almost sunset]." (Luke 23:54)

7. The Women Bought Spices

When did the women buy the spices? There are only two verses that mention the women in connection with the spices they used:

> "And when the sabbath was past, Mary Magdalene, and Mary the *mother* of James, and Salome, had bought ("agorazo," *Strong's* NT#59) sweet spices, that they might come and anoint him." (Mark 16:1)

> "And they returned, and prepared spices and ointments; and rested the sabbath day according to the commandment." (Luke 23:56)

Luke only says that they prepared the spices without saying when they were purchased – it could have been anytime previously. It's possible that Mary Magdalene, after being commended for anointing Jesus for His burial (Matt 26:12), might have thought this through and purchased the spices a few days before they were required. Mark 16:1 could conceivably be saying that at the point they came to anoint Him they had with them the spices that they "had bought," having purchased them some time previously. Here is another passage that uses exactly the same wording (in the Greek) and tense as in Mark 16:1:

> "And they all with one *consent* began to make excuse. The first said unto him, I have bought a piece of ground, and I must needs go and see it: I pray thee have me excused. And another said, I have bought five yoke of oxen, and I go to prove them: I pray thee have me excused." (Luke 14:18-19)

In these cases, the people are saying that they had previously made their purchases. Mark saying that they "had bought" the spices could just be saying that it had been done in the past and, to be consistent with what Luke wrote, it must have been some time earlier and previous to the Sabbath, because they first prepared them, then rested. (The phrase "when the sabbath was past" was discussed in Chapter Three.)

Those who promote a Wednesday-crucifixion scenario, argue that there must have been a day (they suggest Friday) between a ceremonial Sabbath, the first day of the Feast of Unleavened Bread on Thursday, and a seventh-day Sabbath, and do it largely on the basis of the purchase of the spices. However, this verse does not say when the spices and ointments were purchased; it could have been a few days before. For more discussion of Jesus' anointing, see *Appendix 6 – Jesus' Anointing*, p. 131.

> The spices were for a simple anointing, not for a complete embalming which Joseph and Nicodemus had already done.

How Long Did All These Events Take?

Look at all the events that happened here between Jesus' death and burial. In sequence, we have:

> The Jews went to Pilate*
> The order to break the legs was returned to Golgotha*
> The thieves' legs were broken
> Joseph went to Pilate*
> Pilate sent for the centurion*
> The centurion reported to Pilate*
> Joseph returned to the cross for Jesus' body*
> Jesus' body was:
>> removed from the cross
>> wrapped in the linen cloth
>> carried to the tomb
>> prepared with the linen and spices
> The tomb was closed and sealed

This would have all taken some time. Each of the items in the list above that is followed by an asterisk involves a trip between Calvary and Pilate's hall. There were several consecutive one-way trips. That distance, as shown on readily-available maps of ancient Jerusalem, was perhaps only ¼ of a mile, but it had to be close, and they had to find Pilate each time and spend a few minutes there. The point is that a number of events had to happen between Jesus' death at 3 pm and His burial before the start of the Sabbath – a period of about three hours. How much time elapsed between the completion of His burial and the start of the Sabbath? It couldn't have been long; perhaps it was only minutes.

The Sabbath Starts; the Resurrection

With the first night of Jesus' time "in the heart of the earth" starting on the Tuesday evening with His betrayal by Judas to the priests, the three days and three nights would end at sunset on Friday evening. It could be that His death shortly before this marked the end of this time since, as we use the expression "death is a sweet release," He would be free from their control at that point. This allows for His resurrection to happen anytime after that and we would have to look for the moment of His resurrection from other information.

We saw from the symbolism of the Feast of First Fruits (p. 54-55) that the wave sheaf was cut just after sunset at the start of the Sabbath and then was prepared to be waved the next morning. This is quite possibly what happened in Jesus' case. Just at, or immediately following sunset, He was resurrected (harvested) with His presentation as the wave sheaf before the Father happening the next morning.

So now we have the three days and three nights ending quite close to the start of the Sabbath. We know from the timing of the women going to the tomb (p. 72-74) that He had already risen before dawn Sabbath morning. The longest He could have been in the tomb then would be very close to twelve hours and the shortest would be measured in minutes.

The Guard Requested

Do you think the Pharisees watched the burial procedure? Of course they did! They knew where the tomb was. I'm sure that some went to Pilate and others stayed behind watching the disciples to make sure they didn't steal the body. That seemed to be their biggest concern:

> "Now <u>the next day, that followed the day of the preparation</u>, the chief priests and Pharisees came together unto Pilate, Saying, Sir, we remember that that deceiver said, while he was yet alive, After three days I will rise again." (Matt 27:62-63)

Notice that the Sadducees were not mentioned as being part of this delegation which is logical since they did not believe in the resurrection. Any claim by the disciples that Jesus had risen would have held no weight with them and they were likely not concerned about it:

> "Then come unto him the Sadducees, which say there is no resurrection ..."
> (Mark 12:18)

When did the next day begin? – Friday at sunset:

> "Command therefore that the sepulchre be made sure until the third day, lest his disciples come by night, and steal him away, and say unto the people, He is risen from the dead: so the last error shall be worse than the first." (Matt 27:64)

> Do you really think that the Pharisees, having gone this far, would have waited through one night to request a guard, even if it was the Sabbath?

Some people suggest that the guard was requested Sabbath afternoon. This would fit with "the next day" but so would Friday evening, and requesting it after the first night had already passed is not logical. If the guard was not posted until Sabbath morning, the disciples could have removed the body during Friday night-early Saturday morning. If the guard had been posted Sabbath afternoon, and the body was later found to be missing the soldiers could have said that it was stolen during the first night before they were on watch, and thus avoid the charge of being asleep on their watch:

> "Pilate said unto them, Ye have a watch: go your way, make *it* as sure as ye can.
> So they went, and made the sepulchre sure, sealing the stone, and setting a watch."
> (Matt 27:65-66)

The stone would have been sealed after the Sabbath started because the priests requested the guard after sunset. Remember, they had a full moon to do all this by. Sealing anything by the Romans was an official, symbolic procedure. Breaking the seal without authorization would have been punishable, probably by death. Sealing the stone was kind of symbolic that Jesus was totally under their control; He would never bother them again. Perhaps He was resurrected at the very moment the tomb was sealed – just a thought. It is also possible, ironically, that by the time the guard was posted and the seal was actually attached, that they sealed an empty tomb.

Why Did the Women Come to the Tomb?

Some people present the argument that the women were coming to embalm Jesus with the spices and therefore it could not have been on the Sabbath, because that would have been a violation of the law. The error in this reasoning is that the women did not come to embalm Him:

> "And when the sabbath was past, Mary Magdalene, and Mary the *mother* of James, and Salome, had bought sweet spices, that they might come and <u>anoint</u> him." (Mark 16:1)

The women were coming to anoint Him, not to embalm Him. There is a difference. He had already been embalmed in the customary way with a hundred pounds of spices; this being an amount fit for royalty. They were not coming to do that again. Read again John 19:39-40:

> "And there came also Nicodemus, which at the first came to Jesus by night, and brought a mixture of myrrh and aloes, about an hundred pound *weight*. Then took they the body of Jesus, and wound it in linen clothes with the spices, as the manner of the Jews is to bury." (John 19:39-40)

We have a record of another event that Jesus referred to as anointing for His burial:

> "She hath done what she could: she is come aforehand to anoint my body to the burying." (Mark 14:8)

There is considerable difference between pouring a little oil to anoint, and the procedure of wrapping a body in strips of cloth with a hundred pounds of preservative material. So their contribution to the memorial of His death was more like our placing of flowers on a grave site, hardly a Sabbath violation.

When Did the Women Come to the Tomb?

> "In the end of the sabbath, as it began to dawn toward the first *day* of the week, came Mary Magdalene and the other Mary to see the sepulchre." (Matt 28:1)

Earlier (p. 37), we found that the phrase translated "the end of the sabbath" would be better translated "the evening of the sabbath." This verse is also interesting because in the Greek it has two occurrences of the Greek word "sabbaton." The first is translated in the King James Version as "sabbath" and the second is translated as "week." Indeed, this is a strange translation! In the second case, as we have already seen, a better translation would be "one of the sabbaths." The sense is that they came before it was light on the first of the Sabbaths after Passover. Continuing in the narrative:

"And, behold, there was a great earthquake: for the angel of the Lord descended from heaven, and came and rolled back the stone from the door, and sat upon it. His countenance was like lightning, and his raiment white as snow: And for fear of him the keepers did shake, and became as dead *men.*" (Matt 28:2-4)

It seems that the earthquake happened as they were arriving at the tomb. The guards were afraid, not from seeing the resurrected Jesus, but because of the appearance of the angel:

"… the angel of the Lord descended from heaven, and came and rolled back the stone from the door, and sat upon it. His countenance was like lightning, and his raiment white as snow: And <u>for fear of him</u> the keepers did shake, and became as dead *men.*" (Matt 28:2-4)

> The angel rolled back the stone so that the women
> could get in, not so that Jesus could get out.

John starts his account a little earlier than Matthew:

"The first *day* of the week cometh Mary Magdalene early, when it was yet dark, unto the sepulchre, and seeth the stone taken away from the sepulchre." (John 20:1)

Mary came to the tomb "when it was yet dark," so this is earlier than Matthew's "… as it began to dawn …" (Matt 28:1). It seems that Mary may have come on her own at first, perhaps planning to meet the others there.

An important point to emphasis here is that the time described as "yet dark" can only be between sunset and the following sunrise. This excludes the possibility of the women coming to the tomb following an afternoon resurrection as discussed in the section "The Wednesday Crucifixion Theory" in Chapter Four. There is no time during what the Bible calls the "morning" part of the day, between sunrise and sunset when it could be called "yet dark."

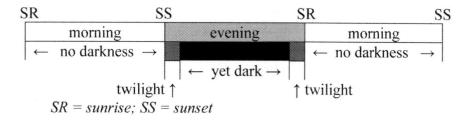

73

If Mary came to the tomb on the day of the resurrection while it was "yet dark" then the resurrection had to have been some time during the preceding dark hours in order for it to have been on the same day. Compare John 20:1 with Mark 16:9 keeping in mind that the word "day" is supplied in both verses. This reasoning applies whichever day the resurrection was on.

The others may have waited for more light but it seems that Mary couldn't wait. She probably couldn't sleep. It says she "seeth the stone taken away from the sepulchre" so there was a little light, obviously enough for her to make her way there. As it was Passover season, there would have been light from a full moon. It does not say she went into the tomb, and probably she could not have seen anything anyway. It says that:

> "Then she runneth, and cometh to Simon Peter, and to the other disciple, whom Jesus loved, and saith unto them, They have taken away the Lord out of the sepulchre, and we know not where they have laid him." (John 20:2)

Note that she came to "Simon Peter, and to the other disciple, whom Jesus loved." Perhaps while she was away to find Peter and John, the other women came. Where were Peter and John? There is a significant clue earlier in John's gospel:

> "Then saith he to the disciple, Behold thy mother! And from that hour that disciple took her unto his own *home*." (John 19:27)

If John took Mary into his home "from that hour" on Friday afternoon, that is where he would have been Sabbath morning. Obviously, Peter was also living or staying there. The other disciples are not mentioned. Evidently, they were elsewhere. A verse that might seem to contradict this is:

> "And when they were come in, they went up into an upper room, where <u>abode</u> both Peter, and James, and John, and Andrew, Philip, and Thomas, Bartholomew, and Matthew, James *the son* of Alphaeus, and Simon Zelotes, and Judas *the brother* of James."
> (Acts 1:13)

This verse includes Peter and James with those who "abode" in the upper room, however, many versions translate the Greek word "meno" (Strong's NT#3306) as "where they were staying." One even translates it as "… where they were waiting…" (*KJ3 Literal Translation*). When you think of it, it is not logical that they would assemble "… for fear of the Jews …" (John 20:19) in one of their homes to which they could be tracked. It was only two days before when they had been directed to the upper room (assuming this is the same room used for their Passover observance), which they did not seem to previously know about.

We can deduce that John did not "live" in the upper room – he had his own home. So the other disciples were then staying in the upper room at a separate location from Peter, John and Mary, Jesus' mother. From John's home, only Peter and John (because they were the only ones of the disciples that were there) are mentioned as running to the tomb, and Mary Magdalene would have followed them back.

By the time Peter and John arrived, there was enough light to see inside the tomb. Entering in they saw the linen clothes and, John writes, speaking of himself, "… he saw, and believed." (John 20:8)

What did he believe? There is no reason to think he did not already believe what Mary had reported to him: "… they have taken away the Lord …" (John 20:2). Some have understood the meaning to be that John, once he saw inside the tomb, believed what Mary had told him, and that is a possible meaning. Further describing their understanding, John says:

> "For as yet they knew not the scripture, that he must rise again from the dead."
> (John 20:9)

To that point, they did not even understand that Jesus would rise again, although He had told them on more than one occasion that He would. John heard Mary say that Jesus had been taken away (John 20:2), but we are not told at that point that he believed anything. He would have seen that the stone had been rolled away, he had stooped down from outside the tomb and saw how the linen clothes were lying (John 20:5), but again it is not recorded that he believed at those moments. When he finally followed Peter in, at that point, "he saw, and believed." (John 20:8). When he went in and had a close look he saw something that caused him to believe. Evidently, he believed something as a result of what he saw, that he did not believe before he saw it. Read *Appendix 7 – "He Saw and Believed"* p. 132 and you'll learn something very interesting about the very unusual and unique thing he saw that made him believe. It does not say whether Peter believed or not but, remember, this is John's account and he is relating his own belief based on what he saw. In all the descriptions about the disciples learning of Jesus resurrection, references to believing are always regarding believing whether He had risen or not, never regarding belief in the suggestion that His body had been stolen.

Then John writes:

> "Then the disciples went away again unto their own home." (John 20:10)

They went to "their own home" suggesting more strongly that Peter and John shared this abode. They would have returned there, at least initially, quite likely to bring the news to Jesus' mother. From there they quite possibly went to join the rest of the disciples. It seems that after Mary followed Peter and John back to the tomb and they had left, she lingered there and this is when Jesus honored her with His first post-resurrection appearance:

> "Now when *Jesus* was risen … he appeared first to Mary Magdalene …"
> (Mark 16:9)

When she recognized Him, He said to her:

> "… Touch me not; for I am not yet ascended to my Father …" (John 20:17)

This indicated that He had not yet ascended to heaven early on Sabbath morning. It seems that Jesus then did ascend quickly to heaven, and return, and then appeared to the other women on their way to the upper room, where He did allow them to touch Him:

> "And as they went to tell his disciples, behold, Jesus met them, saying, All hail.
> And they came and held him by the feet, and worshipped him." (Matt 28:9)

The complete order of events of the different post-resurrection appearances is not easily determined, and will not be dealt with here. We have looked enough at the order of events to show that the resurrection was definitely before sunrise Sabbath morning (and was likely Friday evening at or just after sunset).

As the manna in the wilderness was not found on Sabbath mornings,
the True Manna was not found still "lying on the ground" on Sabbath morning.

More Questions

While we now have a more clear understanding of the chronology, more questions come up. Questions such as:

1. What about the thought that Sabbath-keepers like to point to that Jesus rested in the tomb over the Sabbath?

You will see from *Appendix 8 – Didn't Jesus Rest in the Tomb on Sabbath?* p. 138, that there is no Biblical basis for this idea.

2. What is the impact of this information on the claims for Sunday sacredness?

See *Appendix 9 – There Goes Sunday Sacredness,* p. 139, for the answer. Remember, that the basis for claims of Sunday sacredness is that Jesus rose from the dead on a Sunday.

While this may be the aspect of this study with the greatest implications for Christian practice, it is off the main topic and will be just briefly addressed in the appendix. We want to concentrate here on the deeper meaning of what it meant for Jesus to have been "in the heart of the earth." We have definitely determined from scripture what it is not, but we need to understand better what it is, and what this means for each of us. In Chapter Six, we will look more closely at what it meant for Jesus to have been in "the heart of the earth," and how this helps better our understand of the character of our God.

Chapter 6 – The Thoughts of Many Hearts Revealed

Are the words we say important? You can probably think of words you have said, or words that have been said to you, that have had a great effect in your life. Let's look at some verses of scripture that will bring out the importance of our words and what they reveal about what is in our hearts:

> "Even so the tongue is a little member, and boasteth great things. Behold, how great a matter a little fire kindleth!" (Jam 3:5)

Our words can be what are called cutting words, and do great damage to others:

> "Thy tongue deviseth mischiefs; like a sharp razor, working deceitfully." (Psa 52:2)

Words are important; they have great effect on others and can even affect us as we say them. It is important that we think before we speak:

> "And the tongue *is* a fire, a world of iniquity: so is the tongue among our members, that it defileth the whole body, and setteth on fire the course of nature; and it is set on fire of hell." (Jam 3:6)

> "A man hath joy by the answer of his mouth: and a word *spoken* in due season, how good *is it*!" (Pro 15:23)

> "The heart of the righteous studieth to answer: but the mouth of the wicked poureth out evil things." (Pro 15:28)

Especially important in this study is the fact that words reveal character. The words we speak and how we speak them tell others what we are like, and words spoken in difficult circumstances especially reveal our character. Young people are given the good advice to know someone for two years before marriage. They need to know how their prospective life partner behaves; what they say in difficult circumstances. As we observe people's characters, it is during difficult times that we especially get to know what they are made of.

> Be careful of the thoughts in your heart, they may become
> the words on your lips at any moment.

Now, we are getting closer to the real meaning of the passage of scripture we are focusing on. Naturally, we think at first glance that being "in the heart of the earth" means being in the grave. It has been shown earlier in this study that it means something quite different. It had to, since

Jesus was not dead for three days and three nights. In fact, He was dead for more like only three hours, and in the tomb for perhaps considerably less. We have seen other evidence that refutes the traditional understanding of this passage and there is more to come. We can also consider the context of the passage.

The Sign They Wanted

If we back up in Matthew 12 a few verses from the main passage we are considering, we'll notice something interesting in Jesus' words to the scribes and the Pharisees:

> "Either make the tree good, and his fruit good; or else make the tree corrupt, and his fruit corrupt: for <u>the tree is known by *his* fruit</u>. O generation of vipers, how can ye, being evil, speak good things? for <u>out of the abundance of the heart</u> the mouth speaketh. A good man out of the good treasure <u>of the heart</u> bringeth forth good things: and an evil man out of the evil treasure bringeth forth evil things." (Matt 12:33-35)

> Man's fruit (words and actions) had to be manifest that the
> state of the tree (the heart) might be known.

Jesus makes reference to the heart (in the Greek, "heart" is the same word as He used in the phrase "in the heart of the earth"), saying that the words a man speaks reflect what is in his heart. The words we speak may even have a great influence on our destiny:

> "But I say unto you, That every idle word that men shall speak, they shall give account thereof in the day of judgment. For by thy words thou shalt be justified, and by thy words thou shalt be condemned. Then certain of the scribes and of the Pharisees answered, saying, Master, <u>we would see a sign from thee</u>."
> (Matt 12:36-38)

There is the request – "we would see a sign from thee." What sort of sign did they want? What would have pleased them? The verses just preceding their request were about character. Perhaps what they wanted was a sign that corresponded to their perception of God's character.

Also, the scribes and Pharisees wanted Jesus to perform a miracle at their request and thereby, in a sense, put Him under their control. It was, in part, a question of authority. Note that they did not state their request for a sign in the form of a question. It was not "Jesus, we still have doubts, would you please show us a sign to strengthen our faith?" Rather, it was more like "if you want to be accepted by us and receive our support then we would see a sign from thee, we require undeniable evidence." It was more a demand than a question; a demand based on their concept of their authority over Him, their standing with the people and with God.

It is interesting that Jesus is never recorded as asking anyone for anything. He asked them questions to make them think but, for instance, He didn't ask the woman at the well "Would you please give me some water?" It was "Give me to drink" (John 4:7). In later referring back to what He had said to her:

> "Jesus answered and said unto her, If thou knewest … who it is that <u>saith to thee</u>, Give me to drink …" (John 4:10)

He said "saith to thee," not "asketh of thee." Another example is:

> "… Zacchaeus, make haste, and come down; for to day I must abide at thy house." (Luke 19:5)

> Jesus would not subject Himself to the authority of the religious leaders until the time to do so came in God's plan.

Jesus never used divine power of His own, He relied on His Father to do the works but He always was the Son of God and never relinquished His authority as such. When Satan tempted Jesus in the wilderness to turn the stones into bread (Matt 4:3) it <u>was</u> a temptation because He <u>did</u> have the authority, and the power was available to Him to do it.

The request "we would see a sign from thee" was, in fact, about character. They wanted a "vengeance-is-mine" type of sign. It had to do with their perception of God's character. They wanted a sign to show God's control over man, and one that would also maintain their position of power. And so they asked for a sign. In fact, they had already seen signs – lots of them, undeniable signs. Later, they said of Him:

> " … What do we? for this <u>man</u> doeth many <u>miracles</u>." (John 11:47)

So they were not looking for just another example of healing the downtrodden of society, the ones they considered cursed and forsaken of God. In their eyes, those people were unworthy of God's attention, much less His favor. Such a healing was not the sort of sign they wanted.

The Sign Jesus Offered

Jesus answered the request for a sign by saying:

> "… An evil and adulterous generation seeketh after a sign; and there shall <u>no sign be given to it, but</u> the sign of the prophet Jonas: For as Jonas was three days and three nights in the whale's belly; so shall the Son of man be three days and three nights <u>in the heart</u> of the earth." (Matt 12:39-40)

Jesus obviously understood their request to be more than just for a common miracle. Both of the words "miracle" and "sign" in the two passages quoted above are from the same Greek word "semeion" (Strong's NT#4592). While He had performed many miracles, many of which had been witnessed by them, He specified that there would be one sign only. Notice that He said, " … No sign but …" That doesn't mean "no sign." It means no sign except one, and one only. They demanded a sign, and He said He would give them a sign, but He specified the sign that would be given. The question is: a sign of what? What was Jesus' intent about the sort of sign He would give? It is often understand to be a sign that He was the promised Messiah, but this cannot be. Let's consider more carefully.

Concerning the question at hand, Jesus said there would be <u>only one</u> sign. It must therefore be a sign of something for which no other sign had yet been given. When John the Baptist was in prison he sent two of his disciples to Jesus with the question:

> "… Art thou he that should come? or look we for another?" (Luke 7:19)

The expression "he that should come" was a reference to the Messiah. Here are two examples of its use, one by John the Baptist:

> "I indeed baptize you with water unto repentance: but <u>he that cometh</u> after me is mightier than I, whose shoes I am not worthy to bear: he shall baptize you with the Holy Ghost, and with fire:" (Matt 3:11)

> "And the multitudes that went before, and that followed, cried, saying, Hosanna to the Son of David: Blessed is <u>he that cometh</u> in the name of the Lord; Hosanna in the highest." (Matt 21:9)

Jesus kept John's two disciples waiting while He went about His work of healing and comforting every case that was presented to Him. Then He said to them:

> "… Go your way, and tell John what things ye have seen and heard; how that the blind see, the lame walk, the lepers are cleansed, the deaf hear, the dead are raised, to the poor the gospel is preached." (Luke 7:22)

Jesus knew that John would understand that the miracles He worked as He healed, were signs that He was indeed "he that should come." Jesus had earlier applied Old Testament prophecies of the Messiah to Himself as He read in the synagogue:

> "… The Spirit of the Lord is upon me, because he hath anointed me to preach the gospel to the poor; he hath sent me to heal the brokenhearted, to preach deliverance to the captives, and recovering of sight to the blind, to set at liberty them that are bruised, To preach the acceptable year of the Lord." (Luke 4:18-19)

There were many signs that Jesus was the Messiah. The timing was given by Daniel:

"Know therefore and understand, that from the going forth of the commandment to restore and to build Jerusalem <u>unto the Messiah</u> the Prince shall be seven weeks, and threescore and two weeks ..." (Dan 9:25)

There was the sign of His miraculous birth:

"Therefore the Lord himself shall give you a sign; Behold, <u>a virgin shall conceive,</u> and bear a son, and shall call his name Immanuel." (Isa 7:14)

And there were many other signs that Jesus was the Messiah. If Jesus had said that only one sign would be given as evidence <u>of His divinity,</u> then He would have been denying that His other miracles and the fulfilled prophecies were such evidence which, of course, they were. So He must have been speaking of giving one sign and one sign only, not as proof that He was the Messiah, but as evidence of something else. The question is: a sign of what? More detail on the meaning and significance of the sign will be given in Chapter Seven.

The Heart of Man

Let's look more closely at what it means to be "in the heart." It is what is in the heart that is important. Here are a few verses related to the importance of the heart:

"But the LORD said unto Samuel, Look not on his countenance, or on the height of his stature; because I have refused him: for *the LORD seeth* not as man seeth; for man looketh on the outward appearance, but <u>the LORD looketh on the heart.</u>" (1 Sam 16:7)

"Then hear thou from heaven thy dwelling place, and forgive, and render unto every man according unto all his ways, <u>whose heart thou knowest;</u> (for thou only knowest the hearts of the children of men:)" (2 Chr 6:30)

"Son of man, say unto the prince of Tyrus, Thus saith the Lord GOD; <u>Because thine heart is lifted up</u>, and thou hast said, I *am* a God, I sit *in* the seat of God, in the midst of the seas; yet thou *art* a man, and not God, though thou set thine heart as the heart of God:" (Eze 28:2)

"The heart *is* deceitful above all *things*, and desperately wicked: who can know it?" (Jer 17:9)

The sign that would be given them would be a sign about character. It would reveal both what was in the heart of man towards God, and what was in the heart of God towards man.

The verses just before the passage this book focuses on, show how the heart is referred to in reference to character:

"... for out of the abundance of the heart, the mouth speaketh. A good man out of the treasure of the heart bringeth forth good things: an evil man out of the evil treasure bringeth forth evil things." (Matt 12:34-35).

And the difference between the good and evil is clearly shown by contrast. Talk about a contrast! Ultimately, it reaches the point where man is torturing his Creator; the very one who is responsible for his existence. At the same time, the Creator responding with "Father forgive them" (Luke 23:34), has very different emotions in his heart.

> While man was killing his Creator, the Creator was responding with forgiveness. Their hearts couldn't have been more different!

God works to reveal what is in the heart of man. This is not for His knowledge or benefit for:

"... he [Jesus] knew all *men*, And needed not that any should testify of man: for he knew what was in man." (John 2:24-25)

Rather, we need to know what is in our hearts that we may see our true condition and, hopefully, turn to God and truly give Him our hearts. Here are further verses showing that God works to reveal the condition of our hearts:

"I the LORD search the heart, *I* try the reins, even to give every man according to his ways, *and* according to the fruit of his doings." (Jer 17:10)

"Because that which may be known of God is manifest in them; for God hath shewed *it* unto them." (Rom 1:19)

"Therefore judge nothing before the time, until the Lord come, who both will bring to light the hidden things of darkness, and will make manifest the counsels of the hearts: and then shall every man have praise of God." (1 Cor 4:5)

"For the word of God *is* quick, and powerful, and sharper than any twoedged sword, piercing even to the dividing asunder of soul and spirit, and of the joints and marrow, and *is* a discerner of the thoughts and intents of the heart." (Heb 4:12)

> Listen to a person's words in a difficult or stressful situation, and you will learn something about what is in their heart.

Let's consider more closely how Jesus used the word "heart" in the parables He spoke immediately after His dialogue with the scribes and Pharisees, about a sign. The rest of Matthew 12 and all of Matthew 13 contain a number of parables and some uses of the terms "heart" and "earth." We'll do this by looking at another letter from Jonah. Remember, we were introduced to the setting of Matthew 12 by the first letter of Jonah to his friend in Chapter One.

The Heart of the Earth in Jesus' Parables – The Second Letter

Greetings my dearest Julius,

It is now the third sabbath after Passover and fully a year since I last wrote to you. I know, since you are a Roman citizen, that you are not familiar with many of our customs but we count the weeks which are marked off by sabbaths, between Passover and the Feast of Weeks. Again, much has happened since my last letter. The most incredible events have occurred in the last few weeks here in Jerusalem. After I parted with Jesus and his followers at Capernaum more than a year ago, I returned to Jerusalem and, feeling somewhat disillusioned, I just never got around to writing again.

While Jesus was not around Jerusalem until just before this recent Passover, I kept hearing talk of him and could tell that things were coming to a critical point in his relationship to the religious authorities. After he returned to Jerusalem just the week before Passover, things happened very quickly and within the week, unbelievably, he had been arrested, turned over to the Romans and crucified as a criminal! But, Julius, even more incredibly, He is risen from the dead! Yes, sometime in the evening after His crucifixion, before daylight on the first sabbath after Passover, after only a short time in the tomb he arose and passed right through the graveclothes and the solid rock of the tomb. There were even Roman soldiers guarding his tomb at the request of the chief priests and the Pharisees. After Jesus' death, they had watched every move of the disciples as they didn't want Jesus' followers to have any opportunity to take his body and then claim that he had risen from the dead, as they understood he had claimed he would do. Imagine their surprise when the very ones to claim the body of Jesus and remove it from the cross were Nicodemus, one of their own group, and Joseph of Arimathea, who is about the wealthiest man in Jerusalem. Of course, these events have totally changed my attitude and my understanding of Jesus. How could it not when I saw him after his resurrection with my own eyes!

I would like to record and relate to you all the details of the events of that week but first I want to talk to the disciples and get the details of the events – so much happened. And, I have rejoined the group of Jesus' disciples. Perhaps you have already heard some news from other sources. Everyone is talking about these events. So I will save that for another time and promise I won't take a year to write again. Instead, I will continue where I left off in my previous letter.

Remember, I wrote to you about the sabbath day when Jesus healed the man with the withered hand and the other who was possessed, dumb and blind, and how the Pharisees entered into controversy with him and then demanded a sign. They wanted Jesus to give a sign to prove his claim to be from God, but instead Jesus gave them that rather strange answer about the sign of Jonah. While I could not understand that sign at the time, I do now and will explain it.

Well, the same day, after mentioning the sign of Jonah, Jesus went out of the house and sat by the sea side. And great multitudes were gathered together to him. There were so many people crowded around him that He went into a ship and sat, and the whole multitude stood on the shore from where they could see and hear him better. Since I was not one of the fisherman and there was little space in the ship, I stayed on the shore, but from there I could also hear some of the comments and reactions among the people.

That day, Jesus spoke many things to them in parables that seemed to me to be related to the events earlier in the day. He began by saying, "behold, a sower went out to sow and when he sowed some seeds fell by the way side and the fowls came and devoured them. Some fell upon stony places where they had not much earth and quickly they sprouted because they had no depth of earth, and when the sun was up they were scorched and because they had no root they withered away. And some fell among thorns, and the thorns came up and choked them. But others fell into good ground and brought forth fruit, some a hundredfold, some sixtyfold, some thirtyfold. Who has ears to hear, let him hear."

Later, away from the crowd, the disciples came and asked him, "why do you speak to them in parables?" He answered "because it is given to you to know the mysteries of the kingdom of heaven, but to them it is not given. For whosoever has, to him shall be given and he shall have more abundance but whosoever has not, from him shall be taken away even what he has. Therefore speak I to them in parables because they seeing see not and hearing they hear not, neither do they understand. And in them is fulfilled the prophecy of Isaiah which says, 'By hearing ye shall hear and shall not understand and seeing ye shall see and shall not perceive. For this people's heart is waxed gross, and their ears are dull of hearing and their eyes they have closed; lest at any time they should see with their eyes and hear with their ears and should understand with their heart and should be converted and I should heal them.'"

I could understand that Jesus was saying that it is the condition of the heart that is important. He had said this people's heart is waxed gross. It's not that Jesus was trying to keep the meaning a secret; it's that they chose not to understand. Everyone had ears but some chose to disregard what they heard with their ears. Their hearts were not ready or receptive for that which is spiritually discerned; they were not hungering and thirsting after righteousness as even I was starting to do.

Jesus continued, "But blessed are your eyes, for they see and your ears, for they hear. For verily I say unto you, that many prophets and righteous men have desired to see those things which you see and have not seen them and to hear those things which you hear and have not heard them."

I heard some of the comments of the people spoken quietly among them. It seemed to me that they really did not understand, but they at least appreciated that there was some great import to his words. I didn't totally understand it myself at the time but I could perceive that by the soil he was speaking of the heart. People have since referred to this as the parable of the sower but I like to think of it as the parable of the soils. I think that is more appropriate because, as Jesus explained to us later, the sower and the seed is the same in each illustration while the result – reception or rejection of the truth - is entirely dependent on the condition of the soil, representing the condition of the heart of the one hearing the message.

Here is what he said to us, "Hear therefore the parable of the sower. When any one hears the word of the kingdom and doesn't understand it then comes the wicked one and catches away that which was sown in his heart. This is he which received seed by the way side. But he that received the seed into stony places, the same is he that hears the word and immediately with joy receives it. Yet has he not root in himself and endures only for a while for when tribulation or persecution arises because of the word he is offended. He also that received seed among the thorns is he that hears the word and the cares of this world and the deceitfulness of riches choke the word and he becomes unfruitful. But he that received seed into the good earth is he that hears the word and understands it and which also bears fruit and brings forth some an hundredfold, some sixty, some thirty."

Jesus talked much about the heart that day and used the word often, including in that strange phrase "in the heart of the earth." Here he was saying that it all has to do with the acceptance or rejection of the truths he presented, and ultimately, with the acceptance or rejection of him. The condition of each person's heart determines what kind of earth they are, how well the seed will grow in them and what fruit – words and actions - they will produce.

He spoke yet another parable to them saying "The kingdom of heaven is likened unto a man who sowed good seed in his field. But while men slept, his enemy came and sowed tares among the wheat and went his way. But when the blade was sprung up and brought forth fruit, then appeared the tares also. So the servants of the householder came and said to him 'Sir, did not you sow good seed in your field? From where then has it tares?' He said to them, 'An enemy has done this.' The servants said to him, 'Do you want us to go and gather them up?' But he said, 'No, lest while you gather up the tares, you root up also the wheat with them. Let both grow together until the harvest and in the time of harvest I will say to the reapers, Gather together first the tares, and bind them in bundles to burn them but gather the wheat into my barn.'"

Understanding that the soil represents the state of the heart of the hearer, I could see that this second parable was somehow an expansion of the meaning of the first one. Now the field, the soil, is expanded to mean the whole world. I eagerly awaited his explanation.

Then Jesus sent the multitude away, and went into the house and his disciples came unto him, saying, "Declare to us the parable of the tares of the field." He answered and said to them "he that sowed the good seed is the Son of man, the field is the world, the good seed are the children of the kingdom but the tares are the children of the wicked one. The enemy that sowed them is the devil, the harvest is the end of the world and the reapers are the angels. As therefore the tares are gathered and burned in the fire so shall it be in the end of this world. The Son of man will send forth his angels and they will gather out of his kingdom all things that offend and them which do iniquity and will cast them into a furnace of fire where there will be wailing and gnashing of teeth. Then will the righteous shine forth as the sun in the kingdom of their Father. Who has ears to hear, let him hear."

I am now, months later, able to relate this to what he said to the Pharisees earlier when they asked him for a sign and he replied that he would be "three days and three nights in the heart of the earth." He spoke the parables to explain what he meant by that. The heart, of course, which he talked about so much, refers to the mind and each person's conscious acceptance or rejection of truth.

The first parable referred to different types of soil or earth, to represent the condition of different hearts and how receptive they were to his words. Could he ultimately be saying that he would be in the mind of man who would then have to choose whether to accept or reject him? Incidentally, he did often refer to himself as the word. People who have heard him speak always have to think and make up their minds about his words and eventually about him.

The second parable seemed to expand the setting to the whole world. Each man is allowed to develop his own character and those choices will, in large part, determine his destiny. The chief priests definitely had their minds made up about Jesus. I spoke to Peter, a leader among Jesus' disciples, and he related how just after the dinner at Simon's house, two days before passover, Judas, another disciple and the treasurer of the group, had gone to the chief priests and had betrayed Jesus, agreeing to lead them to arrest him in a secluded place away from the crowds. It seemed to me that, from that point on, the religious authorities were determined to silence him forever.

Jonah the prophet was facing death with, from his point of view, no hope of escape from the belly of the whale. Because of his own actions, he was in a circumstance totally beyond his own control. Similarly, Jesus was facing death; he was within the control of man with no hope of escape from their will. The difference was that Jesus voluntarily placed himself in those circumstances; he actually had allowed himself to be within the control or will of man. He was allowing himself to be controlled by those around him. I think this was, in a way, to show how far God is willing to go to allow man to have, and exercise, his own free will.

I think of the teaching Jesus gave us on prayer. He said that in praying to our father in heaven we should say, "Thy will be done in earth, as it is in heaven." It makes sense to me that we should pray for this as I see how little of God's will is done in our earth. So little, as God allows man to exercise his free will rather than imposing his will on us.

Whenever Jesus spoke of the events of that period of three days and three nights he always started with mention of the betrayal. While I now understand that his being in the heart of the earth referred to his being in the control of man, I sensed that there was an even deeper significance than that. Could this have been what Jesus meant by the sign of the prophet Jonah? That his being in the control of man, subject to their wills, figuratively in the heart of the earth, was to show God's attitude towards them as opposed to their idea of God - that he should control man and his actions?

Jesus had earlier said that if he was lifted up from the earth (a reference to crucifixion) he would draw all men to himself. That certainly happened in my case. In my heart, I have made decisions about him and I have since been rebaptized. That is how I understand we are to celebrate his resurrection, by being symbolically dead and buried with him, and then resurrected to a new life to then walk as he walked. He has changed my life.

Julius, just think of this, he died for your sins. What we do with Jesus is a matter of the heart. Give your heart to Him.

Until another time soon Julius, may Yahweh's blessings be upon you.

Your friend, Jonah.

Note that the original KJV word "ground" (Matt 13:23) quoted on page 85 is changed to "earth" in this letter as it is from the same original Greek word "ge" as the word "earth" in the phrase "in the heart of the earth."

"That the Thoughts of Many Hearts May be Revealed"

According to the prophecy uttered by Simeon at the presentation of Jesus as a baby in the temple, Jesus Himself was appointed as a sign and the reason was given:

> "And Simeon blessed them, and said unto Mary his mother, Behold, this child is <u>set</u> for the fall and rising again of many in Israel; and <u>for a sign</u> which shall be spoken against; ... <u>that the thoughts of many hearts may be revealed</u>."
> (Luke 2:34-35)

The *Online Bible Greek Lexicon* gives one meaning of the word translated "set" (Greek "keimai," *Strong's* NT#2749) as:

> "to be (by God's intent) set, i.e. destined, appointed"

Another example of the use of "keimai" is:

> "That no man should be moved by these afflictions: for yourselves know that we are <u>appointed</u> thereunto." (1 Thess 3:3)

In a sense, Jesus Himself, was set or appointed to be a sign. A result of His being a sign would be that many would either fall or rise again. Let's explore what this means. The *Online Bible Greek Lexicon* definition for the word translated "fall" ("ptosis," *Strong's* NT#4431) is: "a falling, downfall." There are only two uses of "ptosis" in the New Testament, the other being:

> "And the rain descended, and the floods came, and the winds blew, and beat upon that house; and it fell: and great was the <u>fall</u> of it." (Matt 7:27)

The Online Bible Greek Lexicon definitions for the word translated "rising again" ("anastasiv," *Strong's* NT#386) are: "a raising up, rising (e.g. from a seat)" and "a rising from the dead." The original word clearly means resurrection in every other one of its 41 uses. This use (in Luke 2:34) less clearly means a resurrection but, using the exclusive contextual meaning in other scriptures that use it, it would be reasonable to take that as the meaning here also.

In a very real sense, He – Jesus - was the sign. Not that a person just looking at Him would say "surely this is the Son of God," but His words and actions (and fulfillment of prophecy) revealed His identity. The decisions each person made in regard to Him would determine whether they would fall (be eternally lost), or rise again (to eternal life) in the resurrection.

> The choices you make in your heart in regard to Christ will determine
> whether you fall (are lost), or rise (to eternal life) in the resurrection.

The prophecy of Simeon also said that He was appointed "for a sign," and even that He would be "a sign which shall be spoken against." It is interesting that the Greek word for "sign" that was used here is the same Greek word used to report what the Pharisees said in Matthew 12:38: "… we would see a <u>sign</u> from thee." The whole question was over the character of God. Jesus in His life, revealed the true character of God. He, in His words and actions, was a sign sent from heaven.

In addition, through the words and actions of those around Him, the thoughts of many other hearts were revealed; not to God who already reads and knows the heart but to man himself. As each man made his decision in regard to Christ they determined whether they would fall (be eternally lost) or rise (be resurrected to eternal life). Our decisions, our attitude towards the loving character of God have very much to do with our eternal destiny. We decide largely on the basis of our assessment of the words Jesus spoke as did Peter:

> "Then Simon Peter answered him, Lord, to whom shall we go? thou hast the words of eternal life." (John 6:68)

"Out of the Abundance of the Heart" – Case Studies

Especially during the three-day-and-three-night time period we learn something of what is in the hearts of the people involved. It is in a crisis that character is best revealed. So let's look at some of the characters involved in this most critical period of Christ's ministry. Each person or group compared Jesus to what was most important in their lives; made a decision in regard to their relationship to Him and thus manifested, in their words and actions, what was in their heart.

1. The Pharisees – Tradition, Power, Influence

Let's start with the Pharisees since they are the ones disputing with Jesus in Matthew 12. The stage for confrontation was set in the opening verses, as they complained to Him about His disciples plucking and eating corn on the Sabbath. They were misinterpreting God's law (as pointed out by Jesus' reply) and thus, by extension, the character of God. Jesus then went into the synagogue and healed the man with the withered hand (v 9-13) which again illustrated the true character of God, and further inflamed the Pharisees hatred of Him. It says:

"Then the Pharisees went out, and held a council against him, how they might destroy him." (Matt 12:14)

> The Pharisees were the conservative party who ran the local synagogues.
> The Sadducees were the more liberal group who dominated in the temple.

Understanding that the word here translated "destroy" does mean to physically kill, and is a different original word from the one Jesus used in reference to His body in John 2:19; helps us to understand that verse – see *Appendix 10 – Destroy This Temple*, p. 141. He then performed a second miracle, healing the man who was possessed, blind and dumb (Matthew 12:22), which they accused Him of performing by the power of Satan. He showed the fault in their accusation and also pointed out that:

"... the tree is known by *his* fruit." (Matt 12:33)

He then said these significant words:

"... out of the abundance of the heart the mouth speaketh." (Matt 12:34)

They answered, "... Master, we would see a sign from thee." (Matt 12:38). We examined this verse in its context at the beginning of this chapter. The Pharisees were mostly concerned about their position and influence over the people. Tradition was very important to them because this helped to maintain the status quo. For the Pharisees, tradition, power and influence were the important factors in their hearts and this left no place for Jesus.

2. Judas – Self-Seeking and Ambitious

Judas was more concerned about his own wealth and position than anything else. Of course, he "had the bag" (John 13:29), and it would seem that, perhaps, he dipped into it for his personal use. He, among the others, was looking for an earthly kingdom and was ambitious for an important position in it. Many of the apostles were probably disappointed that Jesus did not answer the request, "we would see a sign of thee," with another miracle. They may have thought it a misjudgment on Jesus' part. By the betrayal, Judas was possibly trying to force Jesus' hand, to put Him in a position where He would have to show His authority. Judas, along with the other disciples, was looking for a position in the earthly kingdom he expected Jesus to set up. When he saw that it did not work, he repented of his act, attempting to reverse the betrayal:

"Then Judas, which had betrayed him, when he saw that he was condemned, repented himself, and brought again the thirty pieces of silver to the chief priests and elders, Saying, I have sinned in that I have betrayed the innocent blood ..." (Matt 27:3-4)

The repentance though, was more for the loss of his personal goals than for any conviction of moral wrong. The loss of what was most dear to his heart was so devastating to him that he took his own life:

> "And he cast down the pieces of silver in the temple, and departed, and went and hanged himself. (Matt 27:5)

It seems that Judas' heart was consumed with self. Ambition, position and personal gain were all-important to him. In spite of what he did, Jesus treated him with dignity and did not even openly expose him at the Passover meal.

3. Peter – a Fickle Friend

Peter thought he was a loyal-to-the-death friend of Jesus but he didn't know his own heart. When he was questioned about his association with Jesus in a manner he saw as a possible threat, he quickly reacted in a way to defend himself, even at the denial of any relationship to Jesus. However, Peter had seen and been touched by the character of Jesus – Jesus had washed his feet. Peter saw clearly the condition of his own heart:

> "And Peter went out, and wept bitterly." (Luke 22:62)

Jesus had found a place in Peter's heart because Peter had seen and appreciated the demonstration of the true character of God, and saw the contrast to his own. Jesus, early on, had demonstrated His concern for Peter and the other fishermen by working a miracle that had helped to meet their needs:

> "When Simon Peter saw *it*, he fell down at Jesus' knees, saying, Depart from me; for I am a sinful man, O Lord." (Luke 5:8)

In a similar way, if we will behold the character of God, especially as revealed in the Biblical account of Jesus' life on earth, He will find a place in our hearts.

> Do we, like Peter, who said "yet will I not deny thee," still
> need to learn the condition of our own hearts?

Peter, while he had character faults, had observed Jesus day by day and been attracted to Him and was convicted that He was indeed who He claimed to be:

> "From that *time* many of his disciples went back, and walked no more with him. Then said Jesus unto the twelve, Will ye also go away? Then Simon Peter answered him, Lord, to whom shall we go? thou hast the words of eternal life. And we believe and are sure that thou art that Christ, the Son of the living God." (John 6:66-69)

He could see no other option than to follow Jesus. This helped him recover from his failures and not give up as Judas had. By beholding Jesus, Peter's heart had been changed.

After His resurrection, Jesus gave Peter an opportunity to make right his three-time denial by having him make a three-time affirmation of his love for his Master and gave him the responsibility to "feed my sheep." (John 21:15-17)

4. Pilate – Jesus Was in His Hand, not His Heart

Pilate had a unique position in that he had the authority no one else had - to either release Jesus or condemn Him to death:

> "Then saith Pilate unto him, Speakest thou not unto me? knowest thou not that
> I have power to crucify thee, and have power to release thee?" (John 19:10)

Being in the highest position of local authority he was free to decide either way. Once Jesus' case caught his interest, he examined it more carefully, came to a conclusion and publicly announced his decision:

> "Then said Pilate to the chief priests and *to* the people, I find no fault in this man."
> (Luke 23:4)

He even "sought to release him." (John 19:12) Possibly, there was even pity for Jesus in his heart as well as a sense of fairness. The Jews, sensing that Pilate would not condemn Jesus as readily as they had hoped, finally associated releasing Jesus with Pilate's relation to Caesar:

> "… If thou let this man go, thou art not Caesar's friend: whosoever maketh
> himself a king speaketh against Caesar." (John 19:12)

He then felt threatened in regard to what was dear to his heart - his political position - and he decided to sacrifice Jesus rather than risk his own reputation and position. He clearly showed that his position and authority was more important to him, more dear to his heart than fairness or justice:

> "Then delivered he him therefore unto them to be crucified. And they took Jesus,
> and led *him* away." (John 19:16)

> Do we stay away from a full relationship with Jesus because of fear that
> our position or reputation with others might be endangered?

5. The Soldiers – Doing Their Duty

To the soldiers attending the crucifixion, Jesus was just part of a day's work. They treated Him badly, as they would any other condemned person; only they had reason, because of His claims, to mock Him more than others. However, probably every person they had ever crucified had struggled and cursed. Jesus not only made no struggle, He prayed for their forgiveness as they were driving the nails through His flesh. This would have made a deep impression on them. What they did not have in their hearts was the personal malice that the Jewish leaders had towards Jesus. This made it easier for them to impartially observe the events. The centurion, "and they that were with him" (probably the rest of the company of soldiers), finally made a decision in their hearts about His character:

> "Now when the centurion, and they that were with him, watching Jesus, saw the earthquake, and those things that were done, they feared greatly, saying, Truly this was the Son of God." (Matt 27:54)

The hearts of these outwardly-hardened soldiers were more open to receive the truth than many others who witnessed the scenes of that day. The soldiers, with nothing to lose and without that dangerous pride of position, were willing to acknowledge Him.

We will each reveal our characters by our words and actions. How important that we first learn of Jesus' character as revealed especially by His words and actions.

---

6. John – a Loyal Friend

John, in comparison to Peter, was more willing to stay close to Jesus. He referred to himself as "the one whom Jesus loved." This was not to say Jesus didn't love the others, but John had a very strong sense of Jesus' love for him. He took a greater risk than Peter as he went into the palace after Jesus' arrest, even though he was known by the high priest:

> "And Simon Peter followed Jesus, and so did another disciple: that disciple was known unto the high priest, and went in with Jesus into the palace of the high priest." (John 18:15)

There is no record of Peter having been present at the cross. John, however, was right there. John, formerly characterized as one of the "sons of thunder," had become a son of God. Jesus greatly honored John by asking him to care for His mother:

> "When Jesus therefore saw his mother, and the disciple standing by, whom he loved, he saith unto his mother, Woman, behold thy son! Then saith he to the disciple, Behold thy mother! And from that hour that disciple took her unto his own *home*." (John 19:26-27)

John had room in his heart for Jesus and, when asked by Jesus, also made room in his heart and his home for Jesus' mother. John was a good example of how a receptive heart can be changed. This change was brought about by his close association with Jesus, by daily beholding Jesus' character. If we will regularly behold the glory or character of the Lord, it will change us too, to become more like Him:

> "But we all, with open face beholding as in a glass the glory of the Lord, are changed into the same image from glory to glory, *even* as by the Spirit of the Lord." (2 Cor 3:18)

7. Nicodemus – Had Truth in His Heart

Nicodemus was not a personal friend of Jesus; scripture only records that he had met Jesus once and he is always referred to as the one who "came to Jesus by night." But Jesus had shared a most fundamental truth with him. Evidently, this truth had made a deep impression on him and was planted in his heart:

> "For God so loved the world, that he gave his only begotten Son, that whosoever believeth in him should not perish, but have everlasting life." (John 3:16)

> Nicodemus, a Pharisee in trouble with his peers, is only mentioned in John's gospel written much later than the synoptics and likely after his death.

Nicodemus was well-educated and knew the law. A Pharisee himself, he said to the Pharisees who had sent officers to take Jesus prisoner:

> "Doth our law judge *any* man, before it hear him, and know what he doeth?"
> (John 7:51)

With an honest heart himself, he would have understood the law and how it should be lived. When he witnessed the events surrounding Jesus' death and saw Jesus' character tested to the utmost, the truth in his heart grew. As a witness to the crucifixion, when the cross was lifted into place with Jesus on it, he would have recalled the words of Jesus during his night-time interview:

> "And as Moses lifted up the serpent in the wilderness, even so must the Son of man be lifted up:" (John 3:14)

This would have had the effect on him as related in other words of Jesus:

> "And I, if I be lifted up from the earth, will draw all *men* unto me."
> (John 12:32)

Jesus foresaw what was going to happen and had planted a seed in Nicodemus' heart beforehand. That seed bore fruit, and when the crisis came of dealing with Jesus' dead body before Sabbath, he could only do the right thing regardless of any risk to himself. He then, as shared earlier, took a leading role in doing what he could for the One who now had first place his heart.

What About You? What is in Your Heart?

We each need to become informed, to become knowledgeable of Jesus and make the right decision, in our hearts, with regard to Him. Don't be like the majority of the people who were just blind followers of their leadership. When confronted with a decision they cried out:

"His blood be on us, and on our children." (Matt 27:25)

> Ironically, Jesus' blood applied to them was exactly what they needed. However, they were claiming responsibility for, not the merits of His blood.

The sign from the Son of Man is a call for each of us to carefully examine our own heart to see what is there. What is in your heart? What kind of fruit? How do you treat your enemies? How do you react when you are mistreated? The most important question about your heart and mine is: does Jesus have first place there?

Jesus, in a sense, puts Himself within your control as far as what He will do in regard to you:

If you tell Him to go away and leave you alone, He will do it. He never forces His presence on anyone.

If you ignore Him, He has to keep His distance because He will not come uninvited.

If you will invite Him into your heart, He will come in. He has to because He has promised, and He keeps His promises.

If you ask Him to bless you, He will; as far as your actions, governed by your free will, allow Him to.

So whenever in the future, you hear that phrase, "In the Heart of the Earth," think about its deeper significance. It is referring not to being in the grave but to how Jesus was treated by man, how He allowed Himself to be under the control of man. We will see in Chapter Seven how this shows that God does not force the will of man but will always allow him to make his own choices. And the most important choice for you is what you will do in your heart as far as Jesus is concerned. Will you invite Him in? Is the soil or earth of your heart fertile ground to receive the truth and allow it to germinate and grow?

Chapter 7 – The Heart of the Matter

There is still more to be learned from this portion of scripture. However, before we get to the heart of the matter, there is another issue regarding the timing that many would consider to be critical to this study.

Did Jesus Die On the Wrong Day?

If you have carefully followed the timing presented in this book, you will realize that it identifies the crucifixion day as Nisan 15. Many people will have a hard time with that and insist that the crucifixion must have been on Nisan 14 to fulfill the types. However, this question could be turned around for those who believe that the day Jesus died could only be Nisan 14. The question would then be: if Friday was Nisan 14, why did Jesus consider Passover to be on Nisan 13 and eat the meal that evening, actually in the early hours of Nisan 14 and a day earlier than specified in Leviticus 23?

The fact is that Jesus could not observe both the Passover at the prescribed time and be sacrificed as the antitypical Passover Lamb the same day (actually a few hours before the time of the meal). We could debate which was more important for Him: to die as the Passover Lamb at the specified time "between the two evenings" on the afternoon of Passover Day, Nisan 14 or to partake of the Passover meal at the right time in the early evening of Nisan 15 – clearly He could not do both. However, we do not need to debate because, when scripture is carefully examined, it is clear what happened as far as the timing.

> Jesus could not die as the Sacrificial Lamb and, a few hours
> later, institute the Lord's Supper at a Passover meal.

Here is a thought that affects this problem and is probably new to you. Is it possible that, in God's "Plan A," Jesus would have been sacrificed by the high priest at the altar of sacrifice in the temple, as the official Passover lamb was every year or, at least, in some other way, lay down His life there? The penalty for sin is death and Jesus was the Lamb (planned to be) slain from the foundation of the world. But what lamb was ever crucified? Even Abraham's almost-sacrifice of Isaac which typified Christ's sacrifice, on Mt. Moriah, (centuries later, to be the very site of the altar in the temple in Jerusalem), followed the style of animal sacrifices – there was no cruel cross involved.

Plan A would have required acceptance of Jesus as the Messiah, and recognition of His role as the Lamb of God, by the spiritual leadership and the people of Israel. Surely, the Father would have preferred that and did not compel them in any way to reject His Son. While the spiritual leaders should have understood from scripture, even Jesus' closest companions didn't understand His sacrificial role.

Because Jesus was rejected, God's "Plan A" was thwarted. However, God's eternal purpose was still carried out – the sins of the world were atoned for by the death of Jesus. The way it happened was that Jesus arrived in Jerusalem as the Sacrificial Lamb on time on Nisan 10. He was examined and tested as He taught in the temple. On the day (Nisan 14) the Passover lamb was to be sacrificed, had He been accepted as the spotless Lamb of God that He really was, He should have been sacrificed for the sins of the world. Sacrificed in the temple, not executed by crucifixion outside the city walls of Jerusalem as a common criminal.

As we have seen in Chapter Four, Jesus regarded Thursday as Passover Nisan 14, the day when the preparation was to be made for the Passover meal:

> "Then came the day of unleavened bread, when the passover must be killed. And <u>he sent</u> Peter and John, saying, Go and prepare us the passover, that we may eat. (Luke 22:7-8)

He could see that He was being rejected and went ahead with arrangements to share the Passover meal with His close friends. Then "… when the even was come …" (Matt 26:17) they partook of the meal. This was in the early evening hours of Nisan 15, the first day of the Feast of Unleavened Bread. At that meal, He introduced Himself as the fulfillment of key Passover symbols: "… this is my body…" (1 Cor 11:24); "… this is my blood …" (Mark 14:24) and He asked His followers to "… this do in remembrance of me." (1 Cor 11:24)

Later that evening, He was taken prisoner. He was further tested in a series of trials and, even though He was without fault, He was condemned and crucified. Although Jesus' death on Nisan 15 would seem to be a day late, it was the day, because of sectarian differences between liberals and conservatives, when most of the population of Israel expected the Passover lamb to be slain and more people would then recognize Him as the true Passover Lamb.

An interesting note here is that the earthly sanctuary was but a representation of the sanctuary in heaven where Jesus is spoken of as:

> " … an high priest, who is set on the right hand of the throne of the Majesty in the heavens; A minister of the sanctuary, and of the true tabernacle, which the Lord pitched, and not man." (Heb 8:1-2)

Everything in the earthly sanctuary was symbolic of its greater counterpart in the heavenly sanctuary:

> "For Christ is not entered into the holy places made with hands, *which are* the <u>figures of the true</u>; but into heaven itself, now to appear in the presence of God for us:" (Heb 9:24)

Here is a question: where was the equivalent of the earthly altar of sacrifice in the heavenly sanctuary? The altar was where, for centuries, sacrifices were offered, all pointing forward to the true Lamb of God. The answer is that, since the sacrifice of the heavenly system was Jesus, the altar of the heavenly sanctuary was actually the cross of Calvary on earth. It should have been the altar of sacrifice in the temple - the same site where Abraham "offered" his son Isaac.

> Surely, the heavenly sanctuary is on a much greater scale than
> its earthly representation!

Why Would God Allow This?

Why would God allow the crucifixion to occur on a date different than that prefigured in the ceremonial service? Consistent with the main point of this study, God did not force the will of man to follow His plan (more on this shortly). Jesus should have died on Nisan 14. But God allowed man's will to be carried out in the sacrifice of Jesus. The method of sacrifice also was according to the will of man, using a form of execution invented by the Romans. Don't think for a moment that God came up with that! The crucifixion showed what was in the heart of man. The Bible describes man's heart:

> "The heart *is* deceitful above all *things*, and desperately wicked: who can know it?" (Jer 17:9)

> "For from within, out of the heart of men, proceed evil thoughts, adulteries, fornications, murders," (Mark 7:21)

Man's heart was and is, so desperately wicked that it could go so far as to murder his Creator. The same circumstances showed what was in the heart of God:

> "For I know the thoughts that I think toward you, saith the LORD, thoughts of peace, and not of evil, to give you an expected end." (Jer 29:11)

From the people's perspective, Jesus also died for the wrong reason. He died to remove the guilt of the people's sins yet they were claiming the responsibility for His death (" ... His blood be on us ..." Matt 27:25) because they thought He had sinned.

God had a plan for how things should happen. In fact, it seems that plan was set long ago:

> " ... the Lamb slain from the foundation of the world." (Rev 13:8)

While God had a plan A, He did not force His agenda on man. Rather, He allowed man to exercise his free will and do what was in his heart toward His Son for this period of time. The result, in summary, was that Jesus was sacrificed:

On the wrong day - it should have been on Nisan 14, a day earlier
In the wrong place - it should have been at the altar of sacrifice in the temple
In the wrong way - it should have been by the method used for Passover lambs
For the wrong reason - it should have been in acknowledgment of our need for a
    substitute and acceptance that "… God will provide himself a lamb …"
    (Gen 22:8)

Man did not accept God's plan A and instead shamefully sacrificed God's Son on the wrong day, in the wrong place, in the wrong way and for the wrong reasons. How far God is willing to go to allow man to exercise his free will! And yet the result is still the same as in Plan A - His blood is still on us and our children – not for guilt but for our forgiveness if we will accept it. God's eternal purposes never fail.

The Character of God Further Revealed

We saw in Chapter Six, that the circumstances people went through at the time of the crucifixion brought out, through the words they spoke, what was in each of their hearts. We can learn more about a person's character when we observe him or her in a crisis situation. That is when people tend to let their guards down and reveal what they are really like. The matter (the circumstances) shows what is in the heart (really, the mind) of the person (the earth). However, what about Jesus Himself? How did He react in difficult circumstances? What did He say? What can we learn about His character, about what was in His heart during His time of ultimate testing?

We know that God is love. We certainly are not, although our hearts can be changed in that direction by beholding love in others and especially be beholding the love of God. Scripture tells us that God is different from us; His character is far greater than ours:

> "For my thoughts *are* not your thoughts, neither *are* your ways my ways, saith the LORD. For *as* the heavens are higher than the earth, so are my ways higher than your ways, and my thoughts than your thoughts." (Isa 55:8-9)

> "And the LORD passed by before him, and proclaimed, The LORD, The LORD God, merciful and gracious, longsuffering, and abundant in goodness and truth, Keeping mercy for thousands, forgiving iniquity and transgression and sin, and that will by no means clear *the guilty*; visiting the iniquity of the fathers upon the children, and upon the children's children, unto the third and to the fourth *generation*." (Exo 34:6-7)

> "The LORD *is* merciful and gracious, slow to anger, and plenteous in mercy. He will not always chide: neither will he keep *his anger* for ever. He hath not dealt with us after our sins; nor rewarded us according to our iniquities. For as the heaven is high above the earth, *so* great is his mercy toward them that fear him. As far as the east is from the west, *so* far hath he removed our transgressions from us. Like as a father pitieth *his* children, *so* the LORD pitieth them that fear him." (Psa 103:8-13)

Jesus' Words While on the Cross

It is the challenges we face in life that reveal character, they show what is in the heart. Now let's take this and ask: did Jesus undergo difficult circumstances? Jesus showed His character and the character of the Father all through His life. In the gospels we read of many challenges He faced. He had enemies after Him constantly. His followers had many opportunities to get to know Him, to see how He treated people and how He conducted Himself in various situations. But what was He like under the most difficult circumstances? Let's focus on what Jesus said while He was on the cross. What were Jesus' words while He endured the greatest of His trials and what did those words reveal about His character?

> The word crucible – a trying circumstance - is related to the word crucifixion, as is the word excruciating – referring to great pain. Jesus experienced both.

Remember, Jesus said:

> "… out of the abundance of the heart the mouth speaketh." (Matt 12:34)

We have looked at verses that reinforce that idea. But, since Jesus Himself said these words and implied that our words are a test of what is in our heart, let's apply them to the words He spoke. Surely, what He said could tell us something about His character and the character of the One He claimed to represent.

Actually, we can only go by His words at that time. His ability to act, to do good deeds was limited – He was nailed to a cross. So let's examine what He said. He is only recorded as having spoken seven times. Let's go through them one at a time, in the order He spoke them:

1. To Those Hurting Him

> "Then said Jesus, **Father, forgive them; for they know not what they do ...**"
> (Luke 23:34)

Why did Jesus ask His Father to forgive? Jesus must have had forgiveness in His own heart or why would He ask that? If Jesus had vengeance, or His own interests in His heart He would have asked something as suggested by this verse:

> "Thinkest thou that I cannot now pray to my Father, and he shall presently give me more than twelve legions of angels?" (Matt 26:53)

Or, we might even think that He should have said something more like: "Father, please strike them all dead." But He didn't ask that. Rather, He asked for pardon for His persecutors.

Since He claimed to be representing His Father, we could ask: Was He asking the Father to also find forgiveness within His heart? Most people don't realize that the word forgiveness, in the New Testament, is translated from some very different original words. "Charizomai" (*Strong's* NT#5483) is a word that describes what is happening in the heart of the individual doing the forgiving. "Aphiemi" (*Strong's* NT#863) describes what is happening in the heart of the one who is being forgiven.

He could be saying, in a more amplified rendition, something like this:

> "Father, find a way to help these people who don't know what they are doing and don't realize that you have forgiven them. Help them to realize that you have already forgiven (charizomai) them from your heart and to accept that, and feel forgiven (apheimi) in their own hearts." (Luke 23:34, amplified by author.)

When He asked His Father to forgive His tormentors He was not trying to get the Father to feel like forgiving them. The Father already had forgiveness in His heart. Rather, He was asking His Father to help the soldiers to feel like they were forgiven, to realize that God was not going to stop loving them in spite of what they were doing. *The New American Standard Bible* and some others suggest that, in fact, Jesus repeated this saying over and over:

> "But Jesus <u>was saying</u>, 'Father, forgive them; for they do not know what they are doing' And they cast lots, dividing up His garments among themselves."
> (Luke 23:34, New American Standard Bible)

Jesus did not say "Father forgive them" to persuade His Father to forgive but to help the soldiers understand that they were forgiven. Since the words He used had the meaning of the forgivee receiving forgiveness, the soldiers would have understood Jesus to be asking His Father to help them receive forgiveness; to feel forgiven.

If the Father had reason to be upset with anyone it could have been with those who were so badly mistreating His Son. Rather, in His great heart of love, He had only forgiveness (charizomai) for all that were involved.

2. To the Thief

> "And Jesus said unto him, **Verily I say unto thee, To day shalt thou be with me in paradise.**" (Luke 23:43)

These words were spoken to a man who to all appearances had no hope and no future. He would be expected to be in a state of total despair and without any hope. He was going to be dead soon so why would anyone be concerned about his future? But then there is Jesus who looks to be in the same predicament. Why should He care and what could He have done anyway? In fact, Jesus' position was, in a sense, much worse as He was facing the second death. When we breathe our last on this earth, that is only the first death that saint and sinner alike will suffer. Jesus also experienced the second death, the wages of sin, so that we don't have to suffer that final, eternal separation from God.

> The position of the central cross indicated its occupant was the worst offender. Jesus was considered the chief of sinners.

Here is a use of "today" that is similar to that in the verse we are looking at:

> "Turn you to the strong hold, ye prisoners of hope: even to day do I declare *that* I will render double unto thee;" (Zech 9:12)

Zechariah is recording God as declaring to the returned exiles that "even to day" in spite of their circumstances if they will turn to Him He will deliver them, and even return unto them double. In Luke, Jesus is saying to the dying thief that "even today," in spite of the present circumstances, while being executed as a criminal, he could have hope.

Note also that Jesus did not go to paradise that day. It was the next day, after His resurrection, when He said to Mary:

> "...Touch me not; for I am not yet ascended to my Father..." (John 20:17)

The point that should be emphasized here, in connection with what we are looking at, is that Jesus, in the midst of His own intense suffering, took the time to assure a dying thief that he could have eternal life, that he was forgiven.

The repentant thief suffered the consequences of his crimes against human law, but he did not suffer punishment for breaking divine law. Suffering for the sins of the world, Jesus basically said to the dying thief, "I'll take yours, too."

3. To His Mother and the Beloved Disciple

> "When Jesus therefore saw his mother, and the disciple standing by, whom he loved, he saith unto his mother, **Woman, behold thy son!** Then saith he to the disciple, **Behold thy mother**! And from that hour that disciple took her unto his own *home*." (John 19:26-27)

> Here is evidence that John did not live with the other apostles, and a clue as to where Mary Magdalene went to give the first report of the resurrection.

Of course, we understand this as Jesus asking John to care for His mother. The first three things Jesus said were for the benefit of others. The first was addressed to His Father, but for the benefit of those mistreating Him. The second was for the thief who was otherwise without hope. Now He is providing for the care of His mother. Throughout His intense suffering He thought more of others than of Himself:

"Love … does not seek the *things* of itself …"
(1 Cor 13:4-5, *KJ3 Literal Translation*)

If love does not seek its own good, it must seek the good of others. The one word we most associate with a description of God is "love." Then, if God is love, He does not seek His own, but rather the good of others before His own. When God created others He must have known that He would love them more than Himself. This gives us a clue as to what is, and has always been, in His heart. We will talk more about the heart of God later.

4. To His Father

"And about the ninth hour Jesus cried with a loud voice, saying, **Eli, Eli, lama sabachthani?** that is to say, **My God, my God, why hast thou forsaken me?**"
(Matt 27:46)

"My God, My God." This is the only time Jesus addressed His Father in such a way. Every other time He addressed Him as "Father." Why the difference? And the bigger question about this verse is: why would His Father forsake Him?

Why would He address His Father differently? The answer is that He wasn't addressing His Father. He wasn't even really asking a question. What He was doing was quoting from the well-known Psalm 22 which begins:

"My God, my God, why hast thou forsaken me? …" (Psa 22:1)

We need to look carefully at Psalm 22. It is a messianic Psalm that has much to do with the crucifixion. Apparently, quoting the beginning of a psalm was regarded as a reference to the entire psalm. The people of Jesus' day and certainly the leaders knew scripture (even if they didn't properly understand it). They would have heard those words, and perhaps would have started thinking of the rest of Psalm 22 as they stood there watching Jesus on the cross. Here is a relevant verse from it:

"But I *am* a worm, and no man; a reproach of men, and despised of the people."
(Psa 22:6)

He was despised by the people. That is also mentioned in Isaiah Chapter 53, another passage very much associated with the cross:

"He is despised and rejected of men; a man of sorrows, and acquainted with grief: and we hid as it were *our* faces from him; he was despised, and we esteemed him not." (Isa 53:3)

> "…why hast thou forsaken me?" is the only saying of Jesus on the cross recorded by Matthew or Mark. The others are recorded, three each, by Luke and John.

In Matthew 27, just a few verses before Jesus started quoting from Psalm 22, Matthew describes the people doing what that Psalm says they would do:

> "And they that passed by reviled him, wagging their heads." (Matt 27:39)

> "He trusted in God; let him deliver him now, if he will have him: for he said, I am the Son of God." (Matt 27:43)

Imagine the effect. The people were taunting and reviling Him when suddenly He quoted from Psalm 22. As they thought of it, some of them might have made a connection when they came to verses seven and eight, and realized that they had just said the words it predicted they would say.

> "All they that see me laugh me to scorn: they shoot out the lip, they shake the head, *saying*, He trusted on the LORD *that* he would deliver him: let him deliver him, seeing he delighted in him." (Psa 22:7-8)

Some of them must have really wondered! In their minds, they may have continued through the Psalm:

> "My strength is dried up like a potsherd; and my tongue cleaveth to my jaws; and thou hast brought me into the dust of death." (Psa 22:15)

Again, they may have made a connection. Jesus had had nothing to eat or drink and would have lost considerable fluid from loss of blood. Then they would come to the next verse:

> "... they pierced my hands and my feet." (Psa 22:16)

That was pretty obvious. They may also have remembered a statement from Zechariah:

> "And I will pour upon the house of David, and upon the inhabitants of Jerusalem, the spirit of grace and of supplications: and they shall look upon me whom they have pierced ..." (Zech 12:10)

In two more verses they would come to:

> "They part my garments among them, and cast lots upon my vesture." (Psa 22:18)

The soldiers had done exactly that, probably right at the foot of the cross where they were on duty and in the sight of all. Anyone at the scene who went through Psalm 22 in their minds would have likely made some of these connections. Some may have voiced it audibly:

> "Look, the soldiers just divided His garments - it says that in the Psalms too!"

These fulfillments of details of prophecy may have helped many of the witnesses later decide to follow Him.

> "I will declare thy name unto my brethren: in the midst of the congregation will I praise thee." (Psa 22:22)

He is saying here that He would declare His (the Father's) name, or character. One aspect of God's character is His great love; a love that makes it impossible for Him to abandon the objects of His love. It is not like God to abandon His people. Look at these verses:

> "And, behold, I *am* with thee, and will keep thee in all *places* whither thou goest, and will bring thee again into this land; for I will not leave thee ..."
> (Gen 28:15)

> "Be strong and of a good courage, fear not, nor be afraid of them: for the LORD thy God, *he* it is that doth go with thee; he will not fail thee, nor forsake thee."
> (Deut 31:6)

> "For the LORD will not forsake his people for his great name's sake: because it hath pleased the LORD to make you his people." (1 Sam 12:22)

> "And David said to Solomon his son, Be strong and of good courage, and do *it*: fear not, nor be dismayed: for the LORD God, *even* my God, *will be* with thee; he will not fail thee, nor forsake thee ..." (1 Chr 28:20)

Jesus knew these verses. He was going through the awful pain of the cross. He had every physical reason to feel forsaken by His Father. But Jesus knew the character of His Father. And He, of course, has the same character. He would have known the passages quoted above and understood the thoughts of God later expressed by Paul:

> "... I will never leave thee, nor forsake thee." (Heb 13:5)

> It is so much easier to bear pain when we know someone cares
> about us. We all want someone to sympathize with us.

While He knew these promises, He had to struggle against temptation. Thinking of this Psalm would have helped Him, especially when He came to verse 24:

> "For he hath not despised nor abhorred the affliction of the afflicted; neither hath he [the Father] hid his face from him [the Son]; but when he cried unto him, he heard." (Psa 22:24)

Jesus' faith was sustained by what the word of God says about the character of the Father. He probably felt very forsaken; He certainly had reasons to. He was being tempted to the utmost and, by all appearances, He was forsaken yet that did not affect His estimation of the Father's character.

The fourth saying of Jesus that we have just looked at was addressed to His Father but it was also for the benefit of the people standing around. In fact, it is written that He "cried with a loud voice." He spoke in a loud voice so many of the people would hear it. It had the effect of getting them to think of Psalm 22 and see the remarkable ways in which prophecy was being fulfilled before their eyes.

5. To Fulfill Scripture

> "After this, Jesus knowing that all things were now accomplished, that the scripture might be fulfilled, saith, **I thirst**." (John 19:28)

We have seen, in the first four sayings of Jesus on the cross, that they were more for the benefit of others than for Himself. This saying looks, at first, more like Jesus' concern for Himself; almost a complaint.

However, let's look at some important words – important because they help us understand why He said, "I thirst." Those words are right in the verse: "that the scripture might be fulfilled." What scripture? Again, He was quoting from the Psalms:

> "They gave me also gall for my meat; and in my thirst they gave me vinegar to drink." (Psa 69:21)

"Meat" is from the Hebrew "baruth" meaning "bread of consolation," referring to food sympathizers offer to a mourner; its use here emphasizes their hypocrisy.

Was He thirsty? Absolutely: "… my tongue cleaveth to my jaws." (Psa 22:15) But He said "I thirst" not to fulfill His own needs, but "that the scripture might be fulfilled." The next verse in John says:

> "Now there was set a vessel full of vinegar: and they filled a spunge with vinegar, and put *it* upon hyssop, and put *it* to his mouth." (John 19:29)

Once again, what He said was to help those around the cross to understand what was really going on. True to His character, He was thinking more of others than of Himself.

6. It is Finished

> "When Jesus therefore had received the vinegar, he said, **It is finished**: and he bowed his head, and gave up the ghost." (John 19:30)

Why did He say, "it is finished"? Most people would say because it was the end of Jesus' life. However, these words are misunderstood for much the same reason as the words "my god, my god, why have you forsaken me?" which, remember, were quoted from Psalm 22. It is interesting to consider where the phrase "it is finished" might be quoted from. Actually, it is also from Psalm 22, the last verse:

> "They shall come, and shall declare his righteousness unto a people that shall be born, that he hath <u>done</u> *this*." (Psa 22:31)

The word "done" is from the Hebrew word "asah" (*Strong's* OT#6213). This is the same Hebrew word translated "made" in the creation account:

> "Thus the heavens and the earth were finished, and all the host of them. And on the seventh day God ended his work which he had <u>made</u>; and he rested on the seventh day from all his work which he had <u>made</u>." (Gen 2:1-2)

It can have the meaning of something that is complete, a finished work and, of course, the verse above is saying that creation was then finished. So, the "He hath done this" of Psalm 22, is equivalent to Jesus' words "It is finished."

In Psalm 22 and as Jesus applied it, it was used in the sense of the completion of the work of redemption.

7. Into Thy Hands

> "And when Jesus had cried with a loud voice, he said, **Father, into thy hands I commend my spirit**: and having said thus, he gave up the ghost." (Luke 23:46)

These words were quoted from Psalm 31:

> "<u>Into thine hand I commit my spirit</u>: thou hast redeemed me, O LORD God of truth." (Psa 31:5)

In spite of what looked like a hopeless situation, Jesus used the trusting phrase "into thy hands" as He committed Himself to His Father.

Even today, the words "hand" or "hands" are used symbolically to represent control, responsibility or care. For instance, one large insurance company uses the slogan "you're in good hands," meaning that their customers could rest assured in their services. Some medical doctors, after having done all they can for their patient, have been known to say, "the rest is in God's hands." And we might say "it's out of my hands" meaning that a particular situation is beyond our control and there is nothing more we can do about it. Similar wording was used by King David as he cast himself upon the mercy of God:

> "…let me fall now <u>into the hand</u> of the LORD; for very great *are* his mercies: but let me not fall into the hand of man." (1 Chr 21:13)

> Jesus trusted Himself into His Father's care even as He faced the
> second death. Oh, that we could trust Him more!

God's hands are merciful. He provides for all our needs. We can see from Jesus' seventh saying that He had total and complete trust in His heavenly Father. Peter wrote:

> "Who, when he [Jesus] was reviled, reviled not again; when he suffered, he threatened not; but <u>committed *himself*</u> to him that judgeth righteously."
> (1 Pet 2:23)

Last Words

Frequently, the last words of someone who is dying include a message, or testimony to those who are present. Sometimes it is an expression of love toward family and friends, a request to take care of someone who is being left behind, or a message of instruction. Jesus gave all of these types of messages. His words included all of that, but there was no word of complaint or revenge. Everything He did and said was intended for the good of others. Even while going through intense physical suffering and the greatest emotional struggle anyone has ever undergone, He put others before Himself.

We have mentioned the effect of our words on others. Jesus said of His crucifixion:

> "And I, if I be lifted up from the earth, will draw all *men* unto me."
> (John 12:32)

He was lifted up; both physically on the cross, and in the sense that His words and actions were put on display, both for those who were present at the scene and for those who afterwards are able to read the account of what He said and did. What caused the drawing? Was it something about being crucified? No; the crucifixion part, on its own, was repulsive.

It is the knowledge in our minds and appreciation in our hearts of His willingness to go through what He did for us – that is what draws us. But it is more than the fact that He suffered willingly; it is also how He reacted during that suffering. It was what was in His heart; His attitude to those around Him that mattered. And again, remember, Jesus Himself said:

> "O generation of vipers, how can ye, being evil, speak good things? for <u>out of the abundance of the heart the mouth speaketh</u>. A good man out of the good treasure of the heart bringeth forth good things: and an evil man out of the evil treasure bringeth forth evil things." (Matt 12:34-35)

> Jesus took the place of Barabbas whose name was simply son (bar) of the father
> (abba). We are each the son of a father. Jesus took the place of each of us.

Did Jesus' words while on the cross show what was in His heart? I believe they did. Here they are all together:

1. **"… Father, forgive them; for they know not what they do …"** (Luke 23:34) - forgiveness. Jesus wanted them to feel, to know they were forgiven (Greek - apheimi). Remember, the Father had already forgiven them (Greek - charizomai).
2. **"… Verily I say unto thee To day shalt thou be with me in paradise."** (Luke 23:43) - compassion. Jesus greatest concern was for the salvation of others.
3. **"… Woman, behold thy son! … Behold thy mother! …"** (John 19:26-27) - care for others. Jesus cares about our well being in every aspect.
4. **"… My God, my God, why hast thou forsaken me?"** (Matt 27:46) - teaching from scripture. This saying and the next two are quoted from or, at least, alluded to in Psalm 22 (see verses 1, 15 and 31). Jesus always drew attention to the scriptures.
5. **"… I thirst."** (John 19:28)
6. **"… It is finished …"** (John 19:30)
7. **"… Father, into thy hands I commend my spirit …"** (Luke 23:46) - commitment, trust. Jesus recognized the loving character of His Father (and our God); a God and Father with the same character Jesus showed throughout His life.

The words of Jesus while on the cross revealed His character. They were consistent with the aim of His life which was to point people to the loving character of His Father. Let's think about our own words and how we say them. They reveal our character. And while we might try to be careful of our words, we cannot, on our own, change our characters. Fortunately, that is something that can happen as we look to Jesus lifted up on the cross, and dwell on the words He said. As we think about them we can see what was in Jesus' heart for each of us.

The Father Suffered Too

We are not told much about the emotions in the heart of the Father during these events but we can gain an insight from the connection Jesus made between Himself and His Father:

"Jesus saith unto him, Have I been so long time with you, and yet hast thou not known me, Philip? he that hath seen me hath seen the Father; and how sayest thou *then*, Shew us the Father?" (John 14:9)

Jesus, called by Paul "the image of the invisible God" (Col 1:15), is saying that they have the same character. From this we can deduce that the Father's thoughts towards the people involved in the events of the crucifixion would be the same as those of Jesus. His thoughts would not have been of revenge but more in accord with:

"For I know the thoughts that I think toward you, saith the LORD, thoughts of peace, and not of evil, to give you an expected end." (Jer 29:11)

We are not given much direct insight into the Father's heart at the time of the crucifixion, but we are given a picture through an experience in the life of Abraham. God said to him:

"And he said, Take now thy son, thine only *son* Isaac, whom thou lovest, and get thee into the land of Moriah; and offer him there for a burnt offering upon one of the mountains which I will tell thee of." (Gen 22:2)

For Abraham, the call to sacrifice his son began a time of intense struggle and mental suffering. In the case of Jesus' Father's experience, the Father was withdrawing His protection and allowing the hand-over of Jesus to the control of man, for man to do what was in his heart towards his Creator. In both cases, there would have been great pain in the hearts of the fathers, and for about the same length of time. In the story of Abraham and Isaac, we tend to focus the most on what Abraham would have been feeling, yet we do not consider very much what Jesus' Father was going through. Let's consider a little more the comparison between the two father-son pairs.

Important to note for the purposes of this study is the fact that after Abraham offered his son, he did not have to wait three days to receive him back. And he did, as far as Abraham was concerned, offer him:

"By faith Abraham, when he was tried, offered up Isaac: and he that had received the promises offered up his only begotten *son*," (Heb 11:17)

He had made the decision to obey God's voice to the point "he took the knife to slay his son." (Gen 22:10). Abraham was:

"Accounting that God was able to raise *him* [Isaac] up, even from the dead; from whence [the dead] also he received him in a figure." (Heb 11:19)

So he did, figuratively, receive him from the dead but it wasn't three days later. (See *Appendix 11 - Abraham and Isaac and Three Days*, p. 144)

Thankfully, for this father and son, that sacrifice did not happen, the fire was not kindled; the illustration of what the Heavenly Father would have to go through in giving up His Son was sufficient. This experience would have given Abraham a deep and very personal insight into what would be in the heart of God centuries later, and would have helped him to understand and really appreciate much more the meaning of:

"… God will provide himself a lamb for a burnt offering …" (Gen 22:8)

Here is another thought regarding the length of time Jesus was actually dead. It is often said that this feeling of separation from His Father was so heart–wrenching for Jesus that it broke His heart and caused Him to cry out:

"… My God, my God, why hast thou forsaken me?" (Matt 27:46)

But then, how was it for His Father who had to veil Himself from His only-begotten Son who had taken on the sins of the world – our sins - on behalf of humanity? The separation would have been breaking the heart of the Father also. The Father would have greatly desired to be reunited with His Son. Once the price for sin had been paid and God's love had been demonstrated, why wait? Why delay the resurrection any longer than necessary?

Just as Abraham rejoiced to receive his son back, figuratively, from the dead, the Father would have greatly rejoiced at the resurrection of Jesus. The experience of Abraham and Isaac was an example (a figure) of the trial and the emotional experience that the Father and His Son would later be subject to. It makes sense that the timing would be similar as well. The story of Abraham and Isaac is one more piece of evidence that the three-day-and-three-night time period in question was before the sacrifice, not after.

> Can you imagine any worse emotional struggle than to take or voluntarily give up the life of your own son? Our God of infinite love went through that.

The heart of God has been revealed through His response to what was in the heart of man, in the events surrounding the crucifixion. Understanding this can help us to better recognize and appreciate His love. And God continues to work with each of us in such a way as to show us what is in our own hearts.

A person can choose to follow God and obey His laws because he understands that they are for his best good. A person can choose to proclaim God and to commend His ways to others because he sees improvements and feels better about his own life after becoming a Christian. One can even choose to follow God because of a fear of being lost. However, a person can only choose to follow God as a response of real love from the heart, if he truly understands the love of God towards him. And this can only really be grasped through an appreciation of God's character and the depth of His love:

"We love him, because he first loved us." (1 John 4:19)

Even as we best get to know what a person is really like by observing them in difficult circumstances, the character of God was most clearly revealed in the words and actions of Jesus during His hours on the cross:

"But God commendeth his love toward us, in that, while we were yet sinners, Christ died for us." (Rom 5:8)

We say that God giving His only begotten Son to die on the cross shows His great love for us. It would perhaps be more accurate to say (just as the verse above does), that God giving His only begotten Son to die (omitting mention of the cross) shows His great love for us. How does the cross part (the means of execution that was used) prove God's love? It does not, directly. What the cross shows (not just His death, but how He died) is how far God is willing to go to allow man to have and exercise his free will - which does show His great love for us.

So how does all this relate to the sign of Jonah, and being three days and three nights in the heart of the earth? As mentioned earlier, when Jesus was asked for a sign, He did not deny the request. Rather, He said that a sign would be given, but only one sign, and He specified that the sign was to be the sign of the prophet Jonah. What was that sign? He was not referring back to the incident of Jonah and the whale, and asking them to believe in that. He was talking about a sign that would be given in the future which would be connected with His death and resurrection. What He did was to make comparisons between Jonah's experience and His own. Was it the three days and three nights; was that the important part? We have already seen in Chapter Two that the time period is not even mentioned in some references to the sign of the prophet Jonah. Was it that He would be raised from the dead? Others were raised from the dead and, in the case of Jesus' friend Lazarus, it was even after four days in the grave. If a sign is to signify or provide evidence for a greater truth, it must relate to that truth in some way. How does Jesus being within the control of man for a length of time relate to anything? What greater truth could it be telling us? We need to do some further digging to get to the heart of the meaning of this very important passage of scripture. Let's diverge a little and introduce some new thoughts.

Liar, Lunatic or Lord?

There is a line of reasoning that can be used to persuade a person who is skeptical about who Jesus really was. It goes like this: Jesus was either <u>a liar, a lunatic or the Lord</u> and those are the only three options available. Jesus made claims about Himself, that the Father in heaven was His Father, that He could forgive sin etc. that are consistent with Him being the Lord, the divine, pre-incarnate Son of God. If those claims were not true then He was either consciously lying or He was self-deceived, thinking He was someone He was not, essentially a lunatic. Those people who claim He was just a good man need to consider this reasoning. A "good man" does not go around making false claims and even claiming to be the Son of God. This is much better explained by Josh McDowell in his book *More Than a Carpenter* in which he writes: "I cannot personally conclude that Jesus was a liar or a lunatic. The only other alternative is that he was the Christ, the Son of God, as he claimed." This reasoning was first made popular by C.S. Lewis in his book *Mere Christianity*:

> "I am trying here to prevent anyone saying the really foolish thing that people often say about Him: I'm ready to accept Jesus as a great moral teacher, but I don't accept his claim to be God. That is the one thing we must not say. A man who was merely a man and said the sort of things Jesus said would not be a great moral teacher. He would either be a lunatic — on the level with the man who says he is a poached egg — or else he would be the Devil of Hell. You must make your choice. Either this man was, and is, the Son of God, or else a madman or something worse. You can shut him up for a fool, you can spit at him and kill him as a demon or you can fall at his feet and call him Lord and God, but let us not come with any patronising nonsense about his being a great human teacher. He has not left that open to us. He did not intend to." (Lewis, C. S. *Mere Christianity* 1977. p. 52)

> That Jesus was merely a good man is not an option. People
> need to think this through more thoroughly.

Liar, Lunatic or Like Him?

As this trilemma (like a dilemma but with three choices) challenged the popular view that Jesus was just a great moral teacher, we can use similar reasoning to understand the claims Jesus made about His relationship to His Father. Jesus said things and made claims that, if we believe He is the Lord, have to affect our understanding of the Father. He made statements such as:

"… he that hath <u>seen</u> me hath <u>seen</u> the <u>Father;</u> …" (John 14:9)

Many people look at the Old Testament and see a vengeful God always ready to execute justice. Believers in Jesus see Him as loving and always kind even to His enemies, and certainly wouldn't regard Him as a liar or lunatic. They may even say He is the Lord of their life. If that is so, they cannot rightly regard the character of God and His actions in a way that is entirely inconsistent with the character Jesus portrayed. Similar to the three choices presented previously – <u>liar, lunatic or Lord</u> - the only three available choices here are that Jesus was either <u>a liar, a lunatic or like Him</u> (like His Father). He claimed in several places that He and His Father were of similar character. If they were alike in character their actions must always reflect that likeness.

If that is the case, then we need to seek a different understanding of Old Testament accounts of how God, who claims "… I change not …" (Mal 3:6), treated those that could be called His enemies. Did He actively and personally destroy them or is there another way to understand it? When we look for another way it must, and can only be Biblical, and must be consistent with what we see in the actions of Jesus. As shown already in this book, there are many words for which meanings have changed over the years and translators have allowed traditional beliefs to affect their work. We need to do more than surface read scripture, and we must guard against letting our preconceived ideas affect our understanding.

That the characters of Jesus and His Father are the same and result in similar actions is beyond the scope of this book to explain in detail, but there are a few good publications that lay it out clearly. I would recommend the book *Light on the Dark Side of God* by Marilyn Campbell. She gives logical, scriptural explanations to show that many of the so-called vengeful acts of God in the Old Testament, are not God actively taking vengeance or executing the transgressor. Rather, they are cases of God finally turning from those who have persistently rejected Him, thus removing His protection and allowing the destroyer (Satan) to do his work.

Satan is the Destroyer

"For the LORD will pass through to smite the Egyptians; and when he seeth the blood upon the lintel, and on the two side posts, <u>the LORD</u> will pass over the door, and will not suffer <u>the destroyer</u> to come in unto your houses to smite *you*." (Exo 12:23)

Two individuals are mentioned here; the Lord and the destroyer. The Bible clearly shows that Satan is the destroyer.

> "… I saw a star fall from heaven unto the earth; and to him was given the key of the bottomless pit … And they [the symbolic locusts of verse 3] had a king over them, *which is* the angel of the bottomless pit, whose name in Hebrew tongue *is* <u>Abaddon</u>, but in the Greek tongue hath *his* name <u>Apollyon</u>." (Rev 9:1,11)

Both "Abaddon" and "Apollyon" mean "destroyer." This "fallen star" is identified as Satan:

> "How art thou fallen from heaven, O Lucifer, son of the morning! *how* art thou cut down to the ground, which didst weaken the nations!" (Isa 14:12)

> "And he said unto them, I beheld Satan as lightning fall from heaven." (Luke 10:18)

> "And the great dragon was cast out, that old serpent, called the Devil, and Satan, which deceiveth the whole world: he was cast out into the earth, and his angels were cast out with him." (Rev 12:9)

Isaiah further describes the work of Satan:

> "*That* made the world as a wilderness, and destroyed the cities thereof; *that* opened not the house of his prisoners?" (Isa 14:17)

What is God's Role in Destruction?

Any separation between God and man always begins with man's choice:

> "… The LORD *is* with you, while ye be with him; and if ye seek him, he will be found of you; but <u>if ye forsake him, he will forsake you.</u>" (2 Chr 15:2)

Because God always honors the free will of man, He has no choice but to respect this decision. He forsakes in the sense that - being a gentleman - He does not stay where He is not welcome:

> "Then my anger shall be kindled against them in that day, and I will forsake them, and I will hide my face from them, and they shall be devoured, and many evils and troubles shall befall them; so that they will say in that day, Are not these evils come upon us, <u>because our God *is* not among us</u>? And I will surely hide my face in that day for all the evils which they shall have wrought, in that they are turned unto other gods." (Deut 31:17-18)

God's wrath consists in His turning away or leaving a person to the consequences of their decisions:

> "In a little wrath <u>I hid my face from thee</u> for a moment; but with everlasting kindness will I have mercy on thee, saith the LORD thy Redeemer." (Isa 54:8)

In many Old Testament accounts it can be seen that when God removed His protection and was no longer among His people, then Satan, the destroyer, performed the destruction and, in most cases, managed to cast the blame on God.

God Does Not Use Force

We could legitimately ask the question, "Why didn't God just destroy Lucifer as soon as sin originated in his heart and thus prevent the resulting flood of misery? If He was ever going to use force to remedy a situation it would have made sense to do it at the first sin. Why not just "nip it in the bud" and avoid all the headaches – even avoid the necessity of the cross? The answer is that God wanted to be served only from a heart of love, from intelligent beings using their free wills to choose to serve Him or not. If God always executed His enemies He might get obedience, but it would only be out of fear – there could be no love.

If God would not deny Lucifer's right to choose, then He must similarly honor the free will of mankind. But what about all those Old Testament accounts where God destroyed, participated in the wars of Israel and even told them to kill their enemies? I will give only a very brief explanation here and refer interested readers to the book *Light on the Dark Side of God* mentioned earlier. This book examines case-by-case examples from the Old Testament.

First of all, we need to recognize that it was never God's plan that Israel use arms to occupy the Promised Land:

> "And I will send hornets before thee, which shall drive out the Hivite, the Canaanite, and the Hittite, from before thee." (Exo 23:28)

There is no record of them possessing any arms when they left Egypt. They likely first acquired weapons from the dead Egyptians who washed up on the shore of the Red Sea. Once they had made the decision to take up arms, God had two choices. He could either forcibly remove those arms or somehow prevent Israel from using them, thus violating their free will or He could direct their warfare to minimize the suffering.

The commandment "Thou shalt not kill," and Jesus' teaching and His harmless life, both give evidence of a God that would not destroy. What does not seem to agree is the apparent character of God, as described in Old Testament accounts of God's behaviour, in relation to His enemies. When two witnesses agree and a third does not, it is reasonable to examine the disagreeing witness and see if there can be reconciliation to the others. Jesus said:

> "And he that sent me is with me: the Father hath not left me alone; for I do always those things that please him." (John 8:29)

It does not seem reasonable that the Father would be pleased with Jesus actions while He was on earth, and use contrary actions Himself at other times. By carefully examining Old Testament accounts of apparent divine destruction it can be seen that God merely removed His protection when He was not welcome, and the destroyer, often utilizing the forces of nature, did his work.

The Heart of the Matter

Hopefully, you were able to follow the logic above. You would be richly rewarded by investigating this topic further. Now please follow the reasoning as we see how it connects with the sign of the prophet Jonah, and the three days and three nights that Jesus spent in the heart of the earth. "… God is love …" (1 John 4:8). God created beings upon whom He could bestow that love and who could freely return love to Him. To truly be free to love God they had to also be free to choose not to love Him. They had to be free to choose another way. Obviously, they are not free to do this if they are either incapable (as in pre-programmed robots) or have no opportunity. God went so far as to give Adam and Eve a choice regarding the tree of knowledge of good and evil with all of its potential for sin and destruction. This is good evidence for how far God is willing to go to allow man to have and exercise his free will. As Adam and Eve were, by God's design, free moral agents, He could not restrict their wills to keep them from transgression and yet leave them free. Once they had sinned they had removed themselves, to a great degree, from His protection and the destroyer began his work.

> It is interesting that the "tree of the knowledge of good and evil" could exist in a creation that God Himself proclaimed "very good."

This reasoning is all about the character of God. The debate between Jesus and His listeners in Matthew 12 had much to do with the issue of God's character and it was the big issue in Jesus' life. Throughout His years of ministry on earth, Jesus was constantly attempting to reveal His Father. Consistent with the will and actions of His Father, He never forced the will of anyone under any circumstance:

> "Then answered Jesus and said unto them, Verily, verily, I say unto you, The Son can do nothing of himself, but what he seeth the Father do: for what things soever he doeth, these also doeth the Son likewise." (John 5:19)

God gave man a free will and He will never interfere with it. The ultimate illustration of this, the sign to that wicked and adulterous generation and ours, is that the Father allowed His only-begotten Son to be within the control of man (figuratively, "in the heart of the earth,") for a period of time for man to do with Him as he willed. The Father would not interfere with the will and actions of man even while they tortured and killed His Son.

This understanding of the sign of Jonah is effectively a revelation of a secret code that reveals to us what is in the heart of God – nothing but love for us and a desire for our best good. "Secret," not because it has not always been there, in God's word, but because we have not understood it. It has simply taken some careful investigation of word meanings to uncover the true meaning.

There are a few Biblical examples we could refer to of individuals who were subject to a will other than their own. Jonah himself, for the time he was imprisoned in the whale, was subject to another's will, in his case, through the vehicle of the whale which took Him where He did not want to go. Jesus, for the same length of time, was exposed to a will other than His own – that of His enemies.

Referring to John the Baptist, Jesus (while likening him to Elijah - v13) said:

> "but I say to you that Elijah already came, and they did not recognize him, but did to him whatever they wished. So also the Son of Man is going to suffer at their hands." (Matt 17:12, NASB)

He was saying that they did to John the Baptist whatever they wanted to do. That does not suggest any interference from God to restrict their actions. Rather, it implies they were free to have their way. The Son of Man did not suffer at the hands of His enemies in the same way as John the Baptist in terms of the way He suffered physically. John the Baptist was beheaded, Jesus was crucified. The "so also" was not referring to what they did; not to death in the same way. Rather, it was referring to the fact that to both Jesus and John the Baptist they did "whatever they wished." In both cases, God was allowing man to exercise his free will.

Jesus reference to how Peter would die, commonly understood to be a reference to crucifixion, includes the thought of being carried against his will:

> "Verily, verily, I say unto thee, When thou wast young, thou girdedst thyself, and walkedst whither thou wouldest: but when thou shalt be old, thou shalt stretch forth thy hands, and another shall gird thee, and carry thee whither thou wouldest not." (John 21:18)

In the Garden of Gethsemane, Jesus said:

> "… Father, if thou be willing, remove this cup from me: nevertheless not my will, but thine, be done." (Luke 22:42)

We can reason that it was His Father's will for Jesus to give His life as a ransom for the lost race, as this was necessary for them to be saved. However, it is hardly reasonable to suppose that the Father's will included that His Son should die by crucifixion. But we can see how it could be within the Father's will, as a unique sign to man, that they be allowed to treat His Son according to their own will. It is within the Father's will to allow man to be a free moral agent and make his own choices.

> In God's system we can do whatever we want, we just can't choose
> the consequences – they are connected to the behaviour.

This understanding exalts the character of God and helps us to see Him in a new and brighter light. We could say that God's ultimate objective is to make as many beings as possible, as happy as possible, for as long as possible. This can only be achieved by giving the intelligent beings He created freedom of choice and helping them to be aware of the consequences of their choices. God's approach to us has always been somewhat like that plaque mentioned in the introduction, that I gave to my wife years ago with the saying "Let my love, like sunlight, surround you and yet give you illumined freedom." God wants to give us the desires of our hearts; to allow us to exercise our free wills. While man has, in many ways, rejected God, He still allows us to exercise our free wills. To force our will is really to remove free will. This He will never do but, rather, He seeks to bring us into the sunlight to clearly see His true character and to see that His law is only for our good and happiness. Both David and Paul expressed this understanding of God's law:

> "I delight to do thy will, O my God: yea, thy law *is* within my heart."
> (Psa 40:8)

> "For I delight in the law of God after the inward man:" (Rom 7:22)

In a very real sense, the sign referred to in Matthew 12, allowing Jesus to be "three days and three nights in the heart of the earth," was a demonstration of God's character and manner of dealing with man. He did this because He wants willing - not robotic - allegiance to Himself and He wants us to do that in the full illumination and understanding of His character of love. Through all His responses to the actions of His created beings, and especially during that three-day-and-three-night period when His Son was "in the heart of the earth" it has been shown that, truly, God is love.

List of Appendices

1. Variations in Use of the Word "Even" as in Evening
2. Cases of "Kardia" Translated "Heart" as Understood in this Study
3. Some Thoughts About Inspiration
4. Possible Counts of Days from Feast First Fruits to Pentecost
5. "The Graves of the Saints Were Opened"
6. Jesus' Anointing
7. "He Saw and Believed"
8. Didn't Jesus Rest in the Tomb on Sabbath?
9. There Goes Sunday Sacredness
10. "Destroy this Temple"
11. Abraham and Isaac and Three Days
12. Reference Table of Original Words Investigated

Appendix 1. Variations in Use of the Word "Even" as in Evening

There can be some confusion over the use of the term "even."

> "When the even was come, there came a rich man of Arimathaea, named Joseph, who also himself was Jesus' disciple: He went to Pilate, and begged the body of Jesus. Then Pilate commanded the body to be delivered." (Matt 27:57-58)

"When the even was come" makes it sound like this happened after sunset, and therefore early on the seventh-day Sabbath, Friday evening. But the word "even" was also used in ways other than in reference to what we would call evening, the time after sunset.

> "And ye shall keep it up <u>until the fourteenth day</u> of the same month: and the whole assembly of the congregation of Israel shall kill it in the evening." (Exo 12:6)

Passover lambs were killed in the middle of the afternoon on Nisan 14, prepared and then eaten with unleavened bread after sunset, which is on the first day of the Feast of Unleavened Bread.

> " … there thou shalt sacrifice the passover at even, at the going down of the sun …" (Deut 16:6)

The sun would be visibly seen to be going down (not over the horizon but descending in the sky) after noon. The "in the evening" of Exo 12:6 literally reads, in the original (as the King James Version marginal note says), "between the two evenings." The word "in" used in the phrase "in the evening" is from the Hebrew word "beyn" (*Strong's* OT#996) which is more commonly and better translated as "between" or "betwixt." In fact, of 32 occurrences, this is the only time it is translated as "in." The two evenings are:

1. When the sun begins to visibly descend in the sky (shortly after noon).
2. At sunset when the sun disappears below the horizon (approximately 6 pm).

Gesenius describes "between the evenings" as the time between noon and sunset (Gesenius *Hebrew and Chaldee Lexicon to the Old Testament Scriptures*).

Appendix 2. Cases of "Kardia" Translated "Heart" as Understood in this Study

To help with the correct understanding of the word "heart," as an example of letting the Bible define its own terms, the following verses are listed. They (and many others) use "heart" from the original Greek word "kardia" (*Strong's* NT#2588) in a way that is consistent with this study:

> "O generation of vipers, how can ye, being evil, speak good things? for <u>out of the abundance of the heart the mouth speaketh</u>. A good man <u>out of the good treasure of the heart bringeth forth good things</u>: and an evil man out of the evil treasure bringeth forth evil things." (Matt 12:34-35)

> "When any one heareth the word of the kingdom, and understandeth *it* not, then cometh the wicked *one*, and catcheth away <u>that which was sown in his heart</u>. This is he which received seed by the way side." (Matt 13:19)

> "But those things which proceed out of the mouth <u>come forth from the heart</u>; and they defile the man. For <u>out of the heart proceed</u> evil thoughts, murders, adulteries, fornications, thefts, false witness, blasphemies:" (Matt 15:18-19)

> "For from within, <u>out of the heart of men</u>, proceed evil thoughts, adulteries, fornications, murders," (Mark 7:21)

> "A good man out of <u>the good treasure of his heart</u> bringeth forth that which is good; and an evil man out of the evil treasure of his heart bringeth forth that which is evil: for of the abundance of the heart his mouth speaketh."
> (Luke 6:45)

> "But that on the good ground are they, which in <u>an honest and good heart</u>, having heard the word, keep *it*, and bring forth fruit with patience." (Luke 8:15)

> "And thus are <u>the secrets of his heart</u> made manifest; and so falling down on *his* face he will worship God, and report that God is in you of a truth." (1 Cor 14:25)

These examples all use "kardia" in the sense of the mind, the thinking part of man. We commonly use it that way also but have added other meanings. A good exercise would be to use a concordance to find, and then carefully read every verse that includes a translation from the Greek word "kardia" (*Strong's* NT#2588). Ask yourself if any of them have the meaning of the middle of anything. The context should be considered. If there is only one verse where it is commonly understand to mean that and every other verse has a different meaning, isn't it logical to question the suggested meaning in the one verse, and see if it can be understood with the meaning in all the other verses? This is letting the Bible define its own words.

Appendix 3. Some Thoughts About Inspiration

The conclusions reached in this study, being quite different from the common understanding, might raise a few questions about inspiration itself, so I will attempt to address those here.

We need to be convinced that the word of God is true, that it comes from God and is truly inspired. However, we need to understand just what inspiration means.

This study comes to some surprising conclusions, ones that strongly suggest that the translators of the King James Version were incorrect in one important area, that they were mistaken perhaps because of their preconceived understanding. This is a good example of where we can learn something when we go back to the original version, the one that was originally inspired.

Let's start by considering God's word. The Bible is man's rendition of the inspired word of God. Today it is available in many different versions in a great variety of languages. Which one (or more than one) is inspired? Of course that would have to be the original version, the one written by the Bible writers who were inspired by God. This was written mainly in Hebrew and Greek. Was it inspired word for word? No; the thoughts were inspired, not each individual word. God inspired the different gospel writers to write their recollection of the events of Christ's life. They do not all recount the same events, or even use exactly the same words when quoting a speaker. Even when recording the words of Jesus they sometimes used different wording. But they were still inspired.

The English-language version that we normally think of as an old reliable one, one on which a great deal of today's Christian doctrines are founded, is the King James Version. Its translation into English was completed in 1611 by forty-seven scholars commissioned by King James of England. Is it possible that they might have had some preconceived ideas about scripture, about the events described, and about such things as Sunday sacredness or a Sunday resurrection? Whether or not those ideas influenced their work is another question, but they must have had preconceived ideas – modern Christians surely do! Think of yourself and others you know. It is preconceived ideas that close our minds to other possibilities. It is largely preconceived ideas that result in different doctrines that separate denominations.

> Why should we think that the KJV translators didn't have preconceived ideas that affected their work? They were Bible translators, not Bible writers.

Why wouldn't God allow the King James Version translators to have preconceived ideas? Jesus' own disciples had preconceived ideas about the Messiah and His work and they had those misconceptions even after Jesus Himself had tried to explain the truth to them. God will not take our misconceptions from us. God wants to give us truth but He never forces it. And to those who are willing to dig for truth like treasure, and who will treasure the truth when found, He gives the help needed to find it. God does not and will not control the will of man. I believe this is the highest principle God operates on, other than the principle that God is love. Forcing the will, or somehow making us believe what is right, is just not consistent with love or with God's character.

Concordances

Tools that we use in Bible studies include concordances and lexicons to determine what certain original words mean. However, it is important to realize that the Bible writers did not consult a *Strong's Concordance* or similar reference material to choose words with the right meaning. Rather, James Strong and the authors of other references developed their definitions based on what they perceived the Bible writers to have meant. Of course, this was affected by their theological understanding and the errors already in the translated versions they worked from.

In recent years, computer software has greatly aided Bible study and made it possible to quickly find all the verses using an original word. This makes it much easier to see how the Bible writers used words and thus understand, from the original work itself, the word meanings. That has been one of the major methods used in this study. For example, as discussed in Appendix 2, when every use of the Greek word "kardia" clearly, from the context, has a certain meaning, one can deduce that it may have the same meaning in the one text commonly understood to mean something quite different. When the meaning that is consistent with every other use also, in fact, makes more sense, one has to suspect that the translators may have used it differently in the passage in question, because of their theological background.

> For serious Bible research, a computer program that allows rapid searches and comparisons of Bible versions is invaluable.

How Could God Allow Translations of His Word to Contain any Errors?

We might consider it unthinkable that God would allow men to change even a few words to alter man's understanding of the meaning of the Bible, yet obviously God has allowed man to have His way to a very great extent. In fact, God allowed man to exercise His free will to the point of using about the cruelest means possible to execute His only begotten Son. The major point of this study is that God allowed Jesus to be "in the heart of the earth," within the control of man, to do with Him as they desired, for three days and three nights. The very fact that there are changes in man's translations and versions of God's word, is further evidence for the validity of this study. God gave warnings against changing His word:

> "And if any man shall take away from the words of the book of this prophecy, God shall take away his part out of the book of life, and out of the holy city, and *from* the things which are written in this book." (Rev 22:19)

Why would He have given this warning if He intended to override the free will of the translators to keep their work absolutely consistent with the meaning of the original languages?

Think of it this way. The two most common reasons people will give for believing Jesus was raised on a Sunday would probably be:

1. That is how we and everyone else have always believed it (tradition).
2. That is what my Bible says and it can't be wrong.

But the Bible translators translated it the way they did because they went by the first reason. They simply always believed that the resurrection of Jesus was on the first day of the week because tradition, in their day, supported it. They likely tried their best to do a good job. But they too had preconceived ideas. They had always understood that Jesus was resurrected on Sunday.

Because of traditional ideas, they had an incorrect understanding of which day was the day appointed by God for our weekly day of rest and worship. When they read verses that said, in the Greek, that Jesus rose on Sabbaton, they must have reasoned something like:

"How could it say that (Sabbaton) when He rose on Sunday? There must be a translation issue, another way of understanding the meaning here."

They twisted the meaning, probably without actually meaning to twist scripture, but simply to make it say what they honestly understood it had to mean. And they did it even though the Bible, the original that they translated from, clearly states that the resurrection was on the Sabbath, not the first day of the week. So when we say, "The Bible says it, so I believe it," in some cases we are going by tradition. We are indirectly, following the traditional beliefs of Bible translators who allowed tradition to influence their translation.

False beliefs are sometimes like counterfeit money made by
guilty men, and then circulated unwittingly by honest people.

Does this Make the Bible Unreliable?

It seems that a few changes were made in the translation process by men who thought they were doing the best they could. Of course, we also can go to the same original Hebrew and Greek. If we are willing to set traditional beliefs aside and carefully examine how the Bible itself uses particular words in their contexts, we can come closer to an understanding of the originally intended meaning. This does not take away from the inspiration of God's word. God promised to preserve His word, not our translations or paraphrases of it. Anyone could set out to produce a Bible according to their own understanding of it – that doesn't make it inspired of God. We all know that there are some very questionable translations and paraphrases among the many versions in print.

This book is not meant to shake anyone's faith in God's word. Rather, it is meant to strengthen it and, by using the means mentioned to uncover a hidden truth, encourage deeper study in this and other areas. We need to remember that, with the traditional understanding, we are not looking at God's word as originally given. Rather, what we have, in the case of what Jesus actually said is:

> our understanding (how we, personally, understand it)
> of man's interpretation (generally, the doctrines of today's churches)
> of man's translation (the King James Version or most modern translations)
> of man's written account (the Greek New Testament)
> of Jesus' original words (spoken in Aramaic).

So, really, our understanding is several steps removed from the original words spoken. By going to the original Greek for words with questionable meaning, we are getting considerably closer to the bottom of things, closer to the original meaning and intent of God's word.

> Tradition affects our thinking in very many ways. It can be a strong barrier to open-minded thinking.

Are you struggling to accept the evidence presented here? Think of this. The fact that you are demonstrates how the King James Version translators would have also struggled. They didn't have the tools we do to quickly compare word meanings. Also, they lived in a more traditional, unquestioning culture. Remember, even they lived 1600 years after the events, on the other side of the Dark Ages from the events recorded, and during a time when so much truth was hidden. It is important to carefully examine the evidence and decide from that, not from tradition or preconceived ideas. The King James Version translators (and subsequent translators of other versions) did much good work but it seems that in certain areas, they choose the words to use according to tradition.

The fact is that few people approach the study of God's Word with any effective system of interpretation. They search through the Word and form their own opinions of what they think the passages mean. This is a haphazard and dangerous practice. Allowing the Bible itself to determine the correct meaning of a word is a much safer approach than simply using the definitions of words we already have in our minds. Those who learn and adopt the scriptural method of interpretation largely avoid these problems. They find that contradictions disappear and God's Word comes into complete harmony.

Appendix 4. Possible Counts of the Days from the Feast of First Fruits to Pentecost

The tables following show examples of correct and incorrect determinations of counting the days and weeks between the Feast of Unleavened Bread and Pentecost. In both cases, the day of Passover (Nisan 14) and the First day of the Feast of Unleavened Bread (Nisan 15) are arbitrarily chosen to be the second and third days of the week, a Monday and Tuesday. They could fall on any day of the week in a particular year.

In the incorrect case (Table 1, left), the count starts from the Feast of First Fruits (FFF) which is said to be always on Nisan 16. It starts in this example on a Wednesday (fourth day of the week), includes the seventh day of the Feast of Unleavened Bread (FUB-7) and Pentecost as Sabbaths, and ends up with Pentecost on a Wednesday, for a total count of nine Sabbaths and with the inclusion of part weeks at either end of the fifty days.

In the correct case (Table 2, right), the count starts from the Feast of First Fruits which is always on a seventh-day Sabbath, and ends with Pentecost on a seventh-day Sabbath. There are seven seventh-day Sabbaths, seven full weeks and 50 days.

Comparison of the effect of counting or not counting Feast Days as Sabbaths on the determination of Pentecost.

Table 1. Incorrect. Feasts counted as Sabbaths. Feast of First Fruits on day after "sabbath" (Feast of Unleavened Bread).

Day of 50	Day of week	Feast days	No. of Sabbaths
	2	Pass./Nisan 14	
	3	FUB-1/Nisan 15	
1	4	FFF/Nisan 16	Start count
2	5		
3	6		
4	7		1
5	1		
6	2		
7	3	FUB-7	2
8	4		
9	5		
10	6		
11	7		3
12	1		
~	~		
17	6		
18	7		4
19	1		
~	~		
24	6		
25	7		5
26	1		
~	~		
31	6		
32	7		6
33	1		
~	~		
38	6		
39	7		7
40	1		
~	~		
45	6		
46	7		8
47	1		
~	~		
49	3		
50	4	Pentecost	9

Table 2. Correct. Feasts not counted as Sabbaths. Feast of First Fruits on the seventh-day Sabbath.

Day of 50	Day of week	Feast days	No. of Sabbaths
	2	Pass./Nisan 14	
	3	FUB-1/Nisan 15	
	4		
	5		
	6		
1	7	FFF	Start count
2	1		
3	2		
4	3	FUB-7	
5	4		
6	5		
7	6		
8	7		1
9	1		
~	~		
14	6		
15	7		2
16	1		
~	~		
21	6		
22	7		3
23	1		
~	~		
28	6		
29	7		4
30	1		
~	~		
35	6		
36	7		5
37	1		
~	~		
42	6		
43	7		6
44	1		
~	~		
49	6		
50	7	Pentecost	7

Pass. = Passover; FUB-1 = first day of the Feast of Unleavened Bread; FFF = Feast of First Fruits;
FUB-7 = seventh day of the Feast of Unleavened Bread

Appendix 5. "The Graves of the Saints Were Opened"

Let's consider the timing of the opening of the graves of the saints resurrected with Jesus and when they were resurrected:

> "Jesus, when he had cried again with a loud voice, yielded up the ghost. And, behold, the veil of the temple was rent in twain from the top to the bottom; and the earth did quake, and the rocks rent; And the graves were opened; and many bodies of the saints which slept arose, And came out of the graves after his resurrection, and went into the holy city, and appeared unto many."
> (Matt 27:50-53)

I have always wondered about these verses. It sounds like that at about the same time Jesus died:

> the veil was torn,
> there was an earthquake,
> the rocks rent and
> the graves were opened.

And then it says:

> "and many bodies of the saints which slept arose"
> "and [the bodies] came out of the graves <u>after</u> His resurrection."

The question is: when did the bodies of the saints arise? It was either with the events that happened at His death or with their coming out of the graves which happened later "after His resurrection." It seems that "<u>came out of the graves</u>" is the same event as "<u>bodies of the saints arose</u>." They wouldn't arise before Him – He was the first of the First Fruits:

> "... even so in Christ shall all be made alive. But every man in his own order: Christ the firstfruits; afterward they that are Christ's at his coming."
> (1 Cor 15:22-23)

With the understanding presented in this study, the graves were opened shortly before sunset, at Jesus' death, and the saints came out of their graves sometime after His resurrection which may have been very shortly after sunset. So the graves were physically opened by or at the same time as the earthquake before the resurrection and remained open for perhaps only about three hours before the saints rose shortly after Jesus' resurrection. This makes sense because it is Jesus, the life giver, who wakes the dead:

> "Marvel not at this: for the hour is coming, in the which all that are in the graves shall hear his voice," (John 5:28)

This might also explain what Jesus was doing between His resurrection and when Mary saw Him by the tomb early in the morning. He raised the dead and then may have spent some time instructing them in what to say as they appeared to others in the city. These appearances would have ended by the time Jesus went to heaven to present Himself and these saints to the Father on the Feast of First Fruits, which was on Sabbath morning. We know it was on Sabbath because Jesus observed the Passover on Thursday. Thursday was the Passover, Friday was the first day of the Feast of Unleavened Bread and the Feast of First Fruits was on the seventh-day Sabbath.

Thursday	Friday	Saturday	= Roman days
Fifth Day	Preparation Day	Sabbath Day	= Jewish days of week
Nisan 14	Nisan 15	Nisan 16	= Jewish days of month
Passover Day	Feast of Unleavened Bread	Feast of First Fruits	= Feast days

                    P   D R

P = Passover (Jesus' observance); D = death; R = resurrection

It was seventh-day Sabbath, the Lord's Day, when He ascended and took the resurrected ones with Him to present to the Father:

> "Wherefore he saith, When he ascended up on high, he led captivity captive, and gave gifts unto men." (Eph 4:8)

What gift did He give? He gave the gift of eternal life:

> "For the wages of sin *is* death; but the gift of God *is* eternal life through Jesus Christ our Lord." (Rom 6:23)

He was giving it to those who previously didn't have it; to people who were dead in their graves. The graves were opened in the vicinity of the city of Jerusalem because they "went into the holy city" (Matt 27:53). It is possible that some of the people who were raised were believers who had only recently died; people who had family and friends living who were asking questions about the events surrounding Jesus' death. The raised ones may have visited their relatives, explained recent events and declared that Jesus was risen from the dead, which they could do because they had just seen Him. Their testimony would be convincing because they had just been raised from the dead themselves, and were appearing to people who had recently buried them. Also, they must have been raised early enough on Sabbath to have time to appear and give their testimony to others, before ascending to heaven with Jesus to be presented as the first fruits.

> Other than Moses who was raised from the dead, those raised with Christ were the first to be resurrected and taken to the ultimate Promised Land.

Isaiah suggests a resurrection in connection with Jesus' resurrection:

> "Thy dead *men* shall live, <u>*together with* my dead body shall they arise</u>. Awake and sing, ye that dwell in dust: for thy dew *is as* the dew of herbs, and the earth shall cast out the dead." (Isa 26:19)

Isaiah Chapter 26 starts with a reference to "the land of Judah" and "a strong city" (v1) referring to Jerusalem. "Thy dead *men*" could be referring to inhabitants of Jerusalem and Judah.

Appendix 6. Jesus' Anointing

Jesus was born to be the Messiah; indeed He was "the Lamb (chosen, designated or appointed to be) slain from the foundation of the world" (Rev 13:8). When He was about to enter His work as the Messiah (the word literally means "anointed") at the age of 30, He was anointed at His baptism by John to preach, heal and deliver. That work, for which He was anointed, is described:

> "The Spirit of the Lord *is* upon me, because he hath <u>anointed</u> me to preach the gospel to the poor; he hath sent me to heal the brokenhearted, to preach deliverance to the captives, and recovering of sight to the blind, to set at liberty them that are bruised," (Luke 4:18)

> "How God <u>anointed</u> Jesus of Nazareth with the Holy Ghost and with power: who went about doing good, and healing all that were oppressed of the devil; for God was with him." (Acts 10:38)

There is no mention in those passages about being anointed for His death or burial; it was for His work of preaching, healing, delivering and doing good in many different ways. It was a work of showing what God is really like; a work of representing His Father's character. He was anointed again shortly before His death and burial. This time God used Mary to anoint Him and the anointing is specifically described as being for His burial:

> "She hath done what she could: she is come aforehand to <u>anoint</u> my body to the burying." (Mark 14:8)

John the Baptist of whom Jesus said "there is not a greater prophet than John" (Luke 7:28) anointed Jesus for His role as a prophet. Mary Magdalene, considered a great sinner, anointed Him for His role as sin-bearer and priest.

The Hebrew word for official anointings is "mashach" from which "mashiach" meaning an anointed one or "Messiah" is derived.

It is interesting that the timing of His anointing by Mary coincided with the beginning of the three-day-and-three-night time period. Similarly to Jesus' anointing at the start of His three and a half year work of preaching the gospel, He was again anointed at the start of another phase of His ministry that resulted in His burial three days and three nights later. Once again, we see that the three days and three nights occurred before His death and burial.

Appendix 7. "He Saw and Believed"

We saw, in Chapter Three, the likelihood that Jesus arose at the start of the Sabbath, and I suggested it may even have been when the Roman guard sealed the tomb signifying that He was in their power, that He would never bother anyone again. The Bible never says that the guards saw the resurrected Jesus, only that they were afraid of the angel that rolled away the stone (Matt 28:2-4). But they must have looked inside the tomb and determined that His body was not there or why would the priests persuade them to give a false report to explain its absence?

However, there is still a question, because the women came to the tomb first thing in the morning and we understand that time to be when an earthquake occurred, and an angel opened the tomb in the presence of the soldiers (Matt 28:2). The question is: if Jesus was raised several hours before that, how did He get out of the still-closed tomb through solid rock? The answer from scripture will explain how Jesus got out, why the women were much perplexed at what they saw and what John saw that made him believe.

Burial Customs

In the time of Jesus, burial procedures were well established by traditional religious custom. The Bible says that the common burial method was followed:

> "And there came also Nicodemus, which at the first came to Jesus by night, and brought a mixture of myrrh and aloes, <u>about an hundred pound *weight*</u>. Then took they [Joseph and Nicodemus] the body of Jesus, and wound it in linen clothes with the spices, <u>as the manner of the Jews is to bury</u>." (John 19:39-40)

This "manner of the Jews" involved extensive wrapping of the body with strips of cloth and a considerable amount of an aromatic mixture of myrrh and aloes between the layers. Specifically, John 19:40 says that they "wound it in linen clothes with the spices." Myrrh is the scented gum from a tree which is at first oily, but later hardens as it is exposed to air.

> "In preparing a body for burial according to Jewish custom, it was usually washed and straightened, and then bandaged tightly from the armpits to the ankles in strips of linen about a foot wide. Aromatic spices, often of a gummy consistency, were placed between the wrappings or folds. They served partially as a preservative and partially as a cement to glue the cloth wrappings into a solid covering." (Merrill C. Tenney, *The Reality of the Resurrection*)

> Both Jesus and Lazarus, when buried, would have looked much like mummies are portrayed, wrapped in long strips of cloth.

The story of the raising of Lazarus from the dead helps us:

> "And when he thus had spoken, he cried with a loud voice, Lazarus, come forth. And he that was dead came forth, bound hand and foot with graveclothes: and his face was bound about with a napkin. Jesus saith unto them, Loose him, and let him go." (John 11:43-44)

A few things to observe from this description of Lazarus: he was bound hand and foot. That doesn't mean his hands and feet were tied together; it means he was bound or wrapped in the traditional graveclothes similar to the description above, but right down to his hands and feet. So his arms would have been wrapped also. His legs would have been wrapped separately from each other, or there was no way he would have come forth from the grave on his own. His face was covered by a separate napkin. As he lay in the tomb you wouldn't have seen any part of his body, only its shape covered with all these cloth windings - much like an Egyptian mummy. And the dried myrrh and aloes would have hardened the strips of cloth into a rigid cast.

In some parts of the Middle East, this burial custom is still observed today. In this custom, the head was not wrapped like the rest of the body. A separate "face cloth" or "napkin" was placed over the face. John, describing Jesus' burial mentions this:

> "And the napkin, that was about his head, not lying with the linen clothes, but wrapped together in a place by itself." (John 20:7)

The Shroud of Turin

We are going to come back to the linen clothes but first let's consider the Shroud of Turin. The Shroud of Turin is a single piece of cloth 14 feet long by 3½ feet wide portraying the image of a man who was said to have been wrapped inside it:

> "Tradition claims that it wrapped Jesus' body in the tomb after His crucifixion. Photographic reversal of the lights and shadows of the stains on the shroud … reveals a life-size front and back figure of a man who was crucified, scourged, lanced, and bloodily crowned." (*World Book Encyclopedia*, Vol. 17, p. 362.)

The idea, of course, is that when Jesus came to life, there was something like a blinding flash of light which left His image (as a negative) on the cloth. I am not trying here to establish the much-disputed authenticity of the Shroud of Turin but, to some degree, it fits the events. Let's take a look. When Jesus was dead, Joseph of Arimathea, who was a Pharisee, went to Pilate and requested and received Jesus' body, which was taken down and wrapped in a linen cloth which he had bought:

> "He went to Pilate, and begged the body of Jesus. Then Pilate commanded the body to be delivered. And when Joseph had taken the body, he wrapped it in a clean linen cloth," (Matt 27:58-59)

> Out of respect, Joseph brought a clean linen cloth to use much like a
> body bag, to wrap Jesus' naked body and transport it to the tomb.

Mark 15:46 adds that it was "fine" linen. In John, it tells of someone else that came to help:

> "And there came also Nicodemus, which at the first came to Jesus by night, and brought a mixture of myrrh and aloes, about an hundred pound *weight*. Then took they [Joseph and Nicodemus] the body of Jesus, and wound it in linen clothes with the spices, as the manner of the Jews is to bury." (John 19:39-40)

Joseph and Nicodemus would have carried the body to Joseph's tomb, with it wrapped in the sheet like a body bag. They possibly placed it on a stone slab in the tomb, opened the sheet, wound the body in strips of linen with the spices according to the burial custom and covered it again with the sheet.

Joseph had bought the fine linen cloth. Nicodemus had the spices and he would most likely have had the cloth strips also, everything needed for a burial. In those days, there were no funeral homes. You took care of burying your own loved ones. So, likely there was both the linen sheet and the linen winding cloths to go with the spices. Joseph already had the tomb in preparation for his own burial. Both Joseph ("a rich man of Arimathaea," Matt 27:57) and Nicodemus ("a ruler of the Jews," John 3:1) were wealthy men in Jerusalem, and, if necessary, could have had servants to help.

If you were to have gone into the tomb in that short time between Jesus' burial and resurrection you would have seen a sheet covering the shape of a body, like a person lying in bed, with the sheet pulled up right over the head. Lifting the sheet you would have seen what looked like an Egyptian mummy all wound up and with the face covered with a separate napkin so that none of the body was visible.

What Did Peter and John See?

The Bible says that John, when he went into the tomb, "saw and believed." It seems that at the moment he saw, he believed something that he did not believe before that point. Previously, he did not believe or understand, or even hope that Jesus would be resurrected:

> "For as yet they knew not the scripture, that he must rise again from the dead." (John 20:9)

He had been told by Mary:

> " ... They have taken away the Lord out of the sepulchre, and we know not where they have laid him." (John 20:2)

During Jesus' ministry they had been told what was coming:

"Then he took *unto him* the twelve, and said unto them, Behold, we go up to Jerusalem, and all things that are written by the prophets concerning the Son of man shall be accomplished. ... they shall scourge *him*, and put him to death: and the third day he shall rise again. And they understood none of these things: and this saying was hid from them, neither knew they the things which were spoken. (Luke 18:31,33-34)

In spite of all the reasons for unbelief, something he saw made him believe in the resurrection. And he must have seen something a lot more significant than a pile of graveclothes; it wasn't simply that the body was missing. If he saw just an empty tomb the body could have been stolen. He might then have been accused of stealing the body and his life could be in danger, which would have produced a different reaction.

What did he see? Something very significant, but we need a few other important details first.

"Then the same day at evening, being the first *day* of the week, [remember "first day of the week" is from the Hebrew, meaning more like one of the Sabbaths] <u>when the doors were shut</u> where the disciples were assembled for fear of the Jews, came Jesus and stood in the midst, and saith unto them, Peace *be* unto you." (John 20:19)

"And after eight days again his disciples were within, and Thomas with them: *then* came Jesus, <u>the doors being shut</u>, and stood in the midst, and said, Peace *be* unto you." (John 20:26)

Jesus passed through the solid rock of the unopened tomb as easily
as He did through closed doors to appear to His disciples

Notice that the doors were shut. Jesus must have passed through the walls. When the women arrived at the tomb they saw "that the stone was rolled away" (Mark 16:4). But it was moved for them to get in; it did not have to be moved for Jesus to get out. So what did John and Peter see? Here is what it said they saw:

"Then cometh Simon Peter following him, and went into the sepulchre, and seeth the linen clothes lie, And the napkin, that was about his head, not lying with the linen clothes, but wrapped together in a place by itself." (John 20:6-7)

It says they saw "the linen clothes," not that they saw an empty tomb, not that they saw His body missing. For some reason, there was an emphasis on the linen clothes. There must have been something very significant about that linen. Why was the handkerchief that had been over His face moved to a separate place away from the other graveclothes and why is it even mentioned? They entered the tomb to find Jesus' body missing and, in the process of describing what they saw, talk not about His missing body but about the grave cloths – there had to be something very remarkable about those grave cloths.

What John saw convinced him that there was no way the body could have been stolen. It does not say whether Peter believed or not. What did John see that made him believe? I believe He would have seen what was essentially an empty cast. The pieces of cloth mixed with myrrh and aloes would have dried and formed a somewhat rigid and perhaps not very flexible covering. And also, perhaps, he saw the image on the linen sheet that we now know as the Shroud of Turin. Again, I am not taking a side in the Shroud Controversy. It is just interesting to see how it could fit in.

Think about it. Think about the possibilities: If John had just seen an empty tomb – no body, no graveclothes - he would have thought the body was stolen. If he had seen the graveclothes scattered about or folded up he would still have thought the body was stolen. The graveclothes are mentioned in a way that indicates there was something significant about their appearance that was enough to convince him that Jesus had risen. It would have been impossible to remove the body without either also taking the cloth windings with it or without first unwinding them from the body.

What if the napkin about the face was still in place? He would have thought the body was still there. Just like the rock was moved so the women could get into the tomb, the napkin that covered Jesus' face was moved so that Peter and John could see that the cast was empty. Had it not been moved they would have not even known that He was gone, because the rigid linen cast would have still retained the form of His body. They likely would have been too respectful to move the cloths, and touching a dead body would made them ritually unclean.

Let's examine a little more closely the verses mentioning the clothes to look for clues as to what Peter and John saw. Luke describes what Peter saw and his reaction:

> "Then arose Peter, and ran unto the sepulchre; and stooping down, he beheld the <u>linen clothes</u> (othonion, *Strong's* NT#3608) laid (keimai, *Strong's* NT#2749) by themselves (monos, *Strong's* NT#3441), and departed, wondering (thaumazo, *Strong's* NT#2296) in himself at that which was come to pass." (Luke 24:12)

Some versions more accurately translate "othonion" to show that it referred to the strips of linen used to wrap the body:

> "But Peter got up and ran to the tomb; stooping and looking in, he saw the <u>linen wrappings</u> only; and he went away to his home, marveling at what had happened."
> (Luke 24:12, *NASB*)

> "But Peter got up and ran to the tomb. He bent down and saw only the <u>strips of linen cloth</u>; then he went home, wondering what had happened."
> (Luke 24:12, *The Net Bible*)

According to a footnote for the word "othonion" in the *Net Bible*:

> "In the New Testament this term is used only for strips of cloth used to wrap a body for burial." (*The Net Bible*, footnote #31 for Luke 24:12)

An examination of the five verses that use the word "othonion" confirm this. It is translated as "linen clothes" in reference to what Jesus was wrapped in in each of Luke 24:12, John 19:40 and John 20:5-7. The verses that talk of Jesus being wrapped in "swaddling clothes" use a different original word.

The linen clothes were "<u>laid</u>" by themselves. The Greek verifies this. The English word "laid" was translated from the Greek word "keimai" (*Strong's* NT#2749), which can mean: "to lie, to be laid; to recline, to be lying, to have been laid down." The word shows a person or a thing to be in a lying position. Another example is:

> "And this *shall be* a sign to you; ye shall find the babe wrapped in swaddling clothes, <u>lying</u>, (keimai, 2749), in the manger." (Luke 2:12)

The similarity between the swaddling clothes, also strips of cloth, used to wrap a new born child, and the burial clothes is interesting.

The wording suggests that the linen clothes were still in the position they were when Jesus lay in them.

Did "<u>by themselves</u>" (monos, Strong's NT#3441) mean the clothes were alone, that there were no other clothes around, or did it mean that there was something lacking that should have been, or previously was with them? The Greek word "monos" is translated, in the King James Version, as: "only" twenty four times, "alone" twenty one times, and "by (one's) self" two times. The *Online Bible Greek Lexicon* gives the definition as: "alone (without a companion), forsaken, destitute of help, alone, only, merely." When the clothes were described as being "by themselves" it was not saying that there were no other clothes around. The idea is that they were there without the body that they formerly were wrapped around – something was missing. This was such a strange sight that Peter left "<u>wondering in himself.</u>"

> "Peter's *wondering* was not a lack of faith, but struggling in an attempt to understand what could have happened." (*The Net Bible*, footnote #33 for Luke 24:12)

Peter was wondering (thaumazo, *Strong's* NT#2296) at the appearance of the winding cloth that Jesus body had been wrapped in. The Greek word "thaumazo is most often translated, in its 47 occurrences in the New Testament, as "marvel" (29 times) and "wonder" (14 times). It is much more than just thinking about something. If the disciples had believed the body to have been stolen, their reaction would have been much more one of fear (that they might be accused of it), than of wonder.

The popular Christian song "He's Alive" has a line of lyrics that says:
"But the winding sheet they wrapped Him in was just an empty shell."

Appendix 8. Didn't Jesus Rest in the Tomb on Sabbath?

The idea that Jesus rested in the tomb over Sabbath sounds good to Sabbath-keepers because, they say, He rested at that time, setting an example for us. However, there is no need for this to establish Sabbath sacredness as that was established during creation week in Eden. But here are a few points to consider:

> The first Sabbath, observed in Eden, involved no death.
> The Sabbath is not meant to be a period of inactivity.
> The Sabbath is primarily designed for fellowship with our Creator.
> How is being dead a rest? It does nothing to rejuvenate the body.
> Sabbath sacredness is firmly established without Jesus resting in the tomb on it.
> Jesus resting in the tomb does not set an example for us.

Jesus referred to Himself and His Father working on the Sabbath for the good of others:

> "But Jesus answered them, My Father worketh hitherto, and I work."
> (John 5:17)

Resting in death is no example for us of how to rest while we are alive. It does not say anywhere in scripture that Jesus <u>rested</u> in the tomb over the Sabbath. There is really no similarity between proper Sabbath observance and being dead.

Death is not resting in the sense of not working for a day and using the time for being close to God or family. We put a big emphasis on the Sabbath being a time for relationships and it is – God puts the same emphasis on it. Yet a dead person cannot relate to anyone.

> There are no Biblical references saying that Jesus rested in the tomb over the Sabbath, and there is no scriptural basis for it.

The Creator spent the Sabbath of creation week visiting with the first Adam, who had just been given life, in the Garden of Eden. On the resurrection Sabbath, the Father was reunited with the second Adam who had just been raised to life from His tomb in another garden. No, the Father was not left to spend a mournful Sabbath in the absence of His Son. Rather, Jesus was presented to the Father with those raised at His resurrection, as the first fruits, and at the right time.

Appendix 9. There Goes Sunday Sacredness

The basis among most Christian denominations for the idea that Sunday is sacred is the belief that Jesus' resurrection happened on a Sunday. Can you see why the understanding of the timing of the resurrection presented here could be important?

He Rose on His Day

Most everyone believes that Jesus rose on a Sunday, but Jesus' resurrection occurred on Sabbaton, the seventh-day Sabbath - as would be expected because the seventh-day Sabbath is God's day throughout the entire Bible, in both the Old and New Testaments. Our Lord was raised from the dead on the day which symbolized a finished work, not upon the day that began the weekly toil. Also, Jesus was resurrected at the beginning of the seventh-day Sabbath which, symbolically, looks forward to the resurrection of the saints at the beginning of the millennium.

In the entire Bible, both Old and New Testaments, God's number is seven, and His day is the Sabbath. He instituted the seventh-day Sabbath at Creation (Gen. 2:1-4). He, Himself, made it holy. This was a Sabbath for all mankind, not for the Jews only. The Sabbath was created thousands of years before there was ever a Jew on the earth. Adam and Eve were not Jewish, yet they kept the seventh-day Sabbath as God ordained.

When the Israelites were in the wilderness, after the exodus from Egypt, God reminded them to keep the Sabbath that He had already initiated at creation. He said:

> "<u>Remember</u> the sabbath day to keep it holy. Six days shalt thou labor and do all thy work: But the seventh day *is* the sabbath of the Lord thy God: *in it* thou shalt not do any work ..." (Exo 20:8-10)

He included this seventh-day Sabbath commandment in the ten commandments, and He wrote it Himself, with His own finger, in stone! It must be important and permanent.

When Jesus came to earth, He worshiped and attended the synagogue on the seventh-day Sabbath:

> "And he came to Nazareth, where he had been brought up: and, as his custom was, he went into the synagogue on the sabbath day, and stood up for to read." (Luke 4:16)

At one point he said:

> " ... The sabbath was made for man, and not man for the sabbath: Therefore the Son of man is Lord also of the sabbath." (Mark 2:27-28)

After His resurrection, Jesus met with His disciples and other followers many times and never once did He ever hint that He had changed His holy day. After Jesus' resurrection, His followers and later Paul, continued to keep the Sabbath:

> "And when the Jews were gone out of the synagogue, the Gentiles besought that these words might be preached to them the next sabbath. … And the next sabbath day came almost the whole city together to hear the word of God." (Acts 13:42, 44)

> "And on the sabbath we went out of the city by a river side, where prayer was wont to be made; and we sat down, and spake unto the women which resorted *thither*." (Acts 16:13)

There is no Biblical evidence whatsoever for the establishment of Sunday, the first day of the week, as a holy day or day of rest. And now, we see that even Jesus' resurrection was not on a Sunday, but was on the seventh-day Sabbath. There goes the basis for Sunday-keeping! There goes Sunday sacredness!

If there had been a change from Sabbath to Sunday, there surely would have been some record of it in the New Testament. Rather, it is silent on the questions of either the observance of Sunday by the apostles, or the Jews persecuting them for keeping it in place of the seventh-day Sabbath.

How Should We Celebrate the Resurrection?

If the church was going to celebrate the resurrection they shouldn't be doing it on Sunday, they should do it on the Feast of First Fruits which, it now turns out, is always on a seventh-day Sabbath. There is a way to celebrate the resurrection given in scripture - that is by baptism:

> "Therefore we are buried with him by baptism into death: that like as Christ was raised up from the dead by the glory of the Father, even so we also should walk in newness of life. For if we have been planted together in the likeness of his death, we shall be also *in the likeness* of *his* resurrection:" (Rom 6:4-5)

Baptism, of course, is an individual act each person does to publicly proclaim that they have accepted Jesus. They identify with His death, burial and resurrection by being symbolically buried in the watery grave and rising to a new life.

Appendix 10. "Destroy this Temple"

Here is a verse that seems to suggest three days from Jesus' death to resurrection:

> "Jesus answered and said unto them, <u>Destroy this temple, and in three days I will raise it up</u>. Then said the Jews, Forty and six years was this temple in building, and wilt thou rear it up in three days? But <u>He spake of the temple of His body</u>." (John 2:19-22)

Isn't that referring to a resurrection three days after His death? Jesus even corrects their misunderstanding that He was referring to the temple building. He is clearly speaking about His body. Again we need to look at word meanings:

The word "destroy" is from the Greek word "luo" (*Strong's* NT#3089) for which the *Online Bible Greek Lexicon* gives the major definitions as:

1) to loose any person (or thing) tied or fastened
2) to loose one bound, i.e. to unbind, release from bonds, set free
3) to loosen, undo, dissolve, anything bound, tied, or compacted together

Its 43 uses in the King James Version are translated into the following words (number of uses in parenthesis): loose (27), break (5), unloose (3), destroy (2), dissolve (2), put off (1), melt (1), break up (1), break down (1).

The one other translation of "luo" into "destroy" in the King James Version is:

> "He that committeth sin is of the devil; for the devil sinneth from the beginning. For this purpose the Son of God was manifested, that he might <u>destroy</u> the works of the devil." (1 John 3:8)

That is "destroy the <u>works</u> of the devil," not destroy or kill the devil. The original word does not mean and is never used with the meaning of "to kill someone." We have come to understand it to mean "to kill" as a result of the way it is translated into English. In all of the verses where the Greek word "luo" is used it is never connected with the death of anyone. Also, it is important to note that Jesus said:

> "Therefore doth my Father love me, because <u>I lay down my life</u>, that I might take it again. <u>No man taketh it from me</u>, but I lay it down of myself. I have power to lay it down, and I have power to take it again. This commandment have I received of my Father." (John 10:17-18)

No one killed Jesus. It was the separation from His Father that caused His death. He laid down His life of His own free will. Other verses which support this are:

> "For even the Son of man came not to be ministered unto, but to minister, and to give his life a ransom for many." (Mark 10:45)

> "I am the good shepherd: the good shepherd giveth his life for the sheep." (John 10:11)

> "As the Father knoweth me, even so know I the Father: and I lay down my life for the sheep." (John 10:15)

Jesus said "Destroy this temple, and in three days I will raise it up." There are four other verses where these words of Jesus were quoted, each time by His enemies:

> "And said, This *fellow* said, I am able to destroy the temple of God, and to build it in three days." (Matt 26:61)

> "And saying, Thou that destroyest the temple, and buildest *it* in three days, save thyself. If thou be the Son of God, come down from the cross." (Matt 27:40)

> "We heard him say, I will destroy this temple that is made with hands, and within three days I will build another made without hands." (Mark 14:58)

> "And they that passed by railed on him, wagging their heads, and saying, Ah, thou that destroyest the temple, and buildest it in three days," (Mark 15:29)

They misunderstood His words, not realizing that "He spake of the temple of His body."

The interesting thing here is that they did not understand Him to be referring to His death, but to the destruction of the temple, which is not "killed."

Each of the four verses above refer to destruction using the word "kataluo" (*Strong's* NT#2647), a variation of the word "luo." "Kataluo" is translated: destroy (9), throw down (3), lodge (1), guest (1), come to nought (1), overthrow (1), dissolve (1). The *Online Bible Greek Lexicon* gives the major definitions as:

1) to dissolve, disunite
   1a) (what has been joined together), to destroy, demolish
   1b) metaph. to overthrow i.e. render vain, deprive of success, bring to naught
   1c) of travellers, to halt on a journey, to put up, lodge (the figurative expression originating in the circumstance that, to put up for the night, the straps and packs of the beasts of burden are unbound and taken off; or, more correctly from the fact that the traveller's garments, tied up when he is on the journey, are unloosed at its end)

There are other, more appropriate words Jesus could have used if He meant what we commonly think the passage means. For example, the Greek word "apollumi," (*Strong's* NT#622) which is translated as "perish" (33 times), "destroy" (26), "lose" (22), "be lost" (5), "lost" (4) and miscellaneous other words (2). An example of its use is:

> "Then the Pharisees went out, and held a council against him, how they might <u>destroy</u> him." (Matt 12:14)

Strong's Concordance defines "apollumi" as:

> "to destroy fully; destroy, die, lose, mar, perish"

Other uses of "apollumi" by Matthew include:

> "And his disciples came to *him*, and awoke him, saying, Lord, save us: we <u>perish</u>." (Matt 8:25)

> "But when the king heard *thereof*, he was wroth: and he sent forth his armies, and <u>destroyed</u> those murderers, and burned up their city." (Matt 22:7)

> "Then said Jesus unto him, Put up again thy sword into his place: for all they that take the sword shall <u>perish</u> with the sword." (Matt 26:52)

Here is a verse from Luke:

> "From the blood of Abel unto the blood of Zacharias, which <u>perished</u> between the altar and the temple: verily I say unto you, It shall be required of this generation." (Luke 11:51)

The word "apollumi" would have been a more suitable word for what Jesus said if He was referring to others killing Him. While the meaning of Jesus' words in John 2:19 was definitely not that they would kill Him, exactly what His meaning was is uncertain. However, if you look at the meanings given by lexicons and compare other verses that use the word "luo," it may be possible to understand it close to the original intent. It is most likely connected to their rejection of Him and His message.

Appendix 11. Abraham and Isaac and Three Days

We sometimes make a comparison between the three days and three nights that Jesus spent "in the heart of the earth" and the third day mentioned in connection with Abraham's near sacrifice of his son Isaac:

> "And he said, Take now thy son, thine only *son* Isaac, whom thou lovest, and get thee into the land of Moriah; and offer him there for a burnt offering upon one of the mountains which I will tell thee of. And Abraham rose up early in the morning, and saddled his ass, and took two of his young men with him, and Isaac his son, and clave the wood for the burnt offering, and rose up, and went unto the place of which God had told him. Then <u>on the third day</u> Abraham lifted up his eyes, and saw the place afar off."
> (Gen 22:2-4)

A question we need to ask about the phrase "on the third day" is: "the third day from when?" It cannot be from the near sacrifice of Isaac. The three days were <u>before</u> they arrived at Mt. Moriah. They must be counted from a previous event; logically from when the command was given to Abraham.

> We can carefully examine the verses and line up the events in Genesis 22 parallel to the events during the three days and three nights in Jesus' situation. (However, note that I am not suggesting that the events of Abraham and Isaac were on the same days of the week.) It could look like this:

Tuesday	Wednesday	Thursday	Friday	Saturday
Nisan 12	Nisan 13	Nisan 14/Pass.	Nisan 15/FUB	Nisan 16/FFF
Third Day	Fourth Day	Fifth Day	Preparation Day	Sabbath Day

Jesus: S/B   D R

		Night 1	Day 1	Night 2	Day 2	Night 3	Day 3	

Isaac: C   S/O

Pass. = Passover; FUB = Feast of Unleavened Bread; FFF = Feast of First Fruits
The Father and His Son Jesus: *S = Simon's feast; B = betrayal; D = death; R = resurrection*
Abraham and his son Isaac: *C = command to offer his son; S = sacrifice (almost) of Isaac;*
O = offering of the ram

We are not told the timing exactly but it seems reasonable to assume that Abraham was told what to do in the evening, made some preparations and left on his journey early the next morning; perhaps before telling his wife what he was doing. We see a similar timing in regards to Abraham sending Hagar and Ishmael from the camp:

"And God said unto Abraham … And Abraham rose up early in the morning, and took bread, and a bottle of water, and gave *it* unto Hagar, putting *it* on her shoulder, and the child, and sent her away …" (Gen 21:12, 14)

That evening and the next morning when Abraham and Isaac left for Moriah would be the first of the three days. They travelled together "with two of his young men" and "then on the third day Abraham … <u>saw</u>" so it still had to be light; it was during the light part of the third day. They journeyed that day from the point they saw Moriah until they reached it. They prepared for the sacrifice and, after Abraham's hand was stayed, it was still light enough for Abraham to see the ram, take and sacrifice it instead of his son.

You may have heard the suggestion that the fact that there were three days here supports that Jesus was three days in the tomb. But that does not fit with the story at all - in Abraham's case the three days were before the almost-sacrifice, not after! What are we thinking? Rather than supporting three days in the tomb for Jesus, this supports the theory presented in this book. In the diagram above, you can see that the betrayal of Jesus by Judas was parallel to the command to Abraham to take his son and sacrifice him.

Appendix 12. Reference Table of Original Words Investigated

Page reference	Most correct word(s) in uses considered[a]	Word in original language	Strong's number	Major translations as reported in Strong's with the number of uses[b]
Hebrew words:				
56	After	Achar	310	after(454), follow(78), afterward(s)(46) ...
120	Between	Beyn	996	between(6), betwixt(5), in(1) ...
56	Morrow	Mochorath	4283	morrow(29), next day(2), next(1)
106	Done	Asah	6213	do(1333), make(653), done(336) ...
53	Sabbath	Shabbath	7676	Sabbath(107), another(1)
53	Sabbath	Shabbathon	7677	rest(8), Sabbath(3)
Greek words:				
41	Week	Hebdomad	Not used	Not used
69	had bought	Agorazo	59	buy, had or have bought etc(28) ...
87	rising again	Anastasis	386	resurrection(39), rising again(1) ...
143	Destroy	apollumi	622	perish(33), destroy(26), lose(22)...
100	forgive	apheimi	863	leave(52), forgive(47), suffer(14) ...
21	earth	ge	1093	earth(188), land(42), ground(18) ...
50	preparation	hetoimazo	2090	prepare(29), make ready(10), provide(1)
40	day	hemera	2250	day(355), daily(15) ...
137	wondering	thaumazo	2296	marvel(29), wonder/-ed/-ing(14) ...
19	heart	kardia	2588	heart(159), broken hearted(1)
142	destroy	kataluo	2647	destroy(9), throw down(3), lodge(1) ...
87,137	set, laid	keimai	2749	lie(9), be laid(6), be set(6) be appointed(1) ...
141	loose	luo	3089	loose(27), break(5), unloose(3), destroy(2)...
74	abide	meno	3306	abide(61), remain(16), dwell(15) ...
20	midst	mesos	3319	midst(41), among(6) ...
40	one	mia	3391	one(62), first(8), a certain(4) ...
22	grave	mnemeion	3419	sepulchre(29), grave(8), tomb(5)
137	by themselves	monos	3441	only(24) alone(21), by themselves(2)
136	linen clothes	othonion	3608	linen clothes(5)
50	preparation	paraskeue	3904	preparation(6)
37	even	opse	3796	in the end(1), even(1), at even(1)
50	before	pro	4253	before(44), above(2), ago(1), ever(1)
50	day before the Sabbath	prosabbaton	4315	the day before the Sabbath(1)
40	first	protos	4413	first(84), chief(9), first day(2) ...
87	fall	ptosis	4431	fall(2)
32	Sabbath	sabbaton	4521	Sabbath day(37), Sabbath(22), week(9)
80	sign, miracle	semeion	4592	sign(50), miracle(23), wonder(3), token(1)
100	forgive	charizomai	5483	forgive(11), give(6) freely give(2) ...

[a] Taking context into account.
[b] Listed by frequency. Ellipses indicate the omission of less-frequently used words.

References

American Standard Version 1901. Thomas Nelson & Sons (Public domain)

Amplified Version Scripture quotations taken from the *Amplified® Bible*, Copyright © 1954, 1958, 1962, 1964, 1965, 1987 by The Lockman Foundation Used by permission. (www.Lockman.org)

Authorized King James Version. World Bible Publishers, Iowa Falls, Iowa.

Bacchiocchi, Samuel, 1995. *God's Festivals in Scripture and History Part 1: The Spring Festivals.* Biblical Perspectives, Berrien Springs, Michigan.)

Brown, Robert K. and Philip W. Comfort. 1990. *New Greek English Interlinear New Testament,* Tyndale House, Carol Stream, Illinois.

Campbell, M.M. 2003. *Light on the Dark Side of God.* Truth For the Final Generation, Caldwell, Idaho. (available at www.oigc.net)

Cheney, Johnston M., Earl D. Radmacher and Stanley A. Ellisen. 1969. *The Life of Christ in Stereo: The Four Gospels Speak in Harmony.* Western Baptist Seminary Press

Darby Version. John Nelson Darby. 1867. *The Gospels, Acts, Epistles, and Book of Revelation: Commonly called the New Testament. A New Translation from a Revised Text of the Greek Original.* (Public domain)

Gesenius, William 1974. *Hebrew and Chaldee Lexicon to the Old Testament Scriptures,* Grand Rapids, Michigan Wm. B. Eerdmans Publishing Company.

Good, Joseph. 1991. *Rosh HaShanah and the Messianic Kingdom to Come.* Hatikva Ministries, Port Arthur, Texas

Green, Jay P., Sr., (Editor) 1982. *Pocket Interlinear New Testament.* Baker Book House, Grand Rapids, Michigan

"He's Alive" words copyright ©1977 by New Pax Music Press , ASCAP

Josephus, Flavius. *Antiquities of the Jews,* Book 2 Chapter15 from http://www.ccel.org/j/josephus/works/JOSEPHUS.HTM

KJ3 Literal Translation quotations were taken from The *KJ3 Literal Translation* 2005 Edition, Sovereign Grace Publishers, Inc. http://sgpbooks.com/

Knoch, A.E.1968. *Concordant Commentary on the New Testament.* Concordant Publishing Concern, 15570 Knochaven Road, Santa Clarita, CA 91387, U.S.A.

Knoch, A. E. *Concordant Literal New Testament,* The Concordant Publishing Concern, 15570 Knochaven Road, Santa Clarita, CA 91387, U.S.A http://www.concordant.org

Lane, Jack M. 2004. *The Wave Sheaf Offering -- The Forgotten Holy Day?* From a Bible study given during the Days of Unleavened Bread, 2004 (http://livingtheway.org/wave2.html)

Lewis, C.S., 1977. *Mere Christianity.* Fount Paperbacks, London

McDowell, Josh, 1977. *More Than a Carpenter.* Tyndale House Publishers Inc. Wheaton, Ill.

Modern King James Bible quotations were taken from the *Modern King James Bible*, Sovereign Grace Publishers, Inc.

New American Standard Bible (NASB) Scripture taken from the *New American Standard Bible*, Copyright © 1960,1962,1963,1968,1971,1972,1973,1975,1977,1995 by The Lockman Foundation. Used by permission.

New International Version Scripture taken from the *Holy Bible, New International Version*. Copyright © 1973, 1978, 1984 International Bible Society. Used by permission of Zondervan. All rights reserved.

Online Bible Greek Lexicon, Online Bible Millennium Edition Version 1.02.02 Timnathserah Inc., Winterbourne, Ontario (www.onlinebible.net)

Strong, James. *Strong's Exhaustive Concordance of the Bible.*

Tenny, Merrill C. 1972. *The Reality of the Resurrection.* Moody, Press, Chicago

Thayer, Joseph. 1885. *Thayer's Greek-English Lexicon of the New Testament.* (Public domain)

The Net Bible www.bible.org/netbible

The Scriptures. 1998. Institute for Scripture Research (Pty) Ltd. South Africa.

World Book Encyclopedia 1977. Field Enterprises Educational Corporation.

Young, Robert. 1898. *Young's Literal Translation* (YLT) Baker Book House, Grand Rapids Michigan. (Public domain)

Scripture Index

Genesis
1:5	12
2:1-2	106
2:1-4	139
3:19	21
21:12, 14	145
22:2	30,109
22:2-4	144
22:8	98,109
22:10	109
28:15	104
50:25	58

Exodus
12:3	58,61
12:3,6	45
12:6	45,61,120
12:8	46,52
12:10	30
12:17	58
12:23	112
13:19	57,58
20:8-10	139
21:6	9
23:28	114
31:15	54
34:22	58
34:6-7	98

Leviticus
23:5-6	46
23:6	52
23:6-8	53
23:10-11	54
23:11	53,56,57
23:11,15,16	54
23:14	55
23:15	39,56,57,59
23:15-16	53,60
23:16	56,57
23:24	53
23:39	53

Numbers
9:12	31
33:3	46,58
33:5	58

Deuteronomy
16:6	120
16:9	58
21:22-23	67
31:6	104
31:17-18	113
32:1	21

1 Samuel
12:22	104
16:7	81

2 Kings
5:27	9

1 Chronicles
21:13	106
28:20	104

2 Chronicles
6:30	81
15:2	113

Nehemiah
13:19	56

Job
34:15	21

Psalms
16:10	29
16:11	xi
18:4-5	18
21:2	xi
22:1	102,108
22:6	102
22:7-8	103
22:15	103,105,108
22:16	103
22:18	103
22:22	104
22:24	104
22:31	106,108
31:5	106
40:8	117
52:2	77
69:21	105

Psalms (cont'd)
88:4,6	18
103:8-13	98
118:26	62

Proverbs
15:23	77
15:28	77

Isaiah
1:2	21
7:14	81
14:12	113
14:17	113
26:19	130
53:3	102
53:7	61
54:8	114
55:8-9	8,98

Jeremiah
17:9	81,97
17:10	82
22:29	21
29:11	97,108

Ezekiel
28:2	81

Daniel
9:25	81
9:27	52

Jonah
1:17	9,12
2:6	9,18

Zechariah
9:9	63
9:12	101
12:10	103

Malachi
3:6	8,112
4:1	9

Scripture Index

Matthew

3:11	80
4:3	79
5:22,28	23
5:39	7
7:11	xi
7:27	87
8:25	143
12:1	42
12:8	44
12:9-13	88
12:14	89,143
12:22	89
12:33	89
12:33-35	78
12:34	89,99
12:34-35	82,107,121
12:36-38	78
12:38	88-9
12:38-40	xii,11
12:39-40	13,79
12:40	15,17,20-1
12:41	26
13:19	121
13:23	87
14:24	20
15:18-19	121
16:4	25
17:12-13	116
17:22-23	22
20:18-19	23
21:8	62
21:9	80
21:18	116
22:7	143
25:41	8
25:46	8
26:2	24,65
26:6	23
26:12	69
26:14-15	23
26:17	48,50-1,96
26:17-20	24,46
26:20	49
26:52	143
26:53	99
26:61	142

Matthew (cont'd)

27:3-4	89
27:5	90
27:25	26,94,97
27:39	103
27:40	142
27:43	103
27:45	66
27:46	66,102,108-9
27:46-50	66
27:50-53	128
27:51-52	66
27:53	129
27:54	67,92
27:57	134
27:57-58	120
27:58-59	133
27:62	50,51
27:62-63	71
27:64	71
27:65-66	71
28:1	34,36-9,51,72-3
28:2-4	73,132
28:9	76

Mark

2:27-28	139
7:21	97,121
10:45	142
11:11	63
11:12	64
11:13-14	64
11:15-16	64
11:19	37,64
11:20	64
11:27	64
11:27-28	64
12:1	64
12:13	64
12:18	64,71
12:28	64
12:34	64
12:35	64
12:37	64
13:1	64
13:35	37

Mark (cont'd)

14:1	64,65
14:3	64
14:8	72,131
14:10	23,64
14:11	49
14:12	40,47,50,64
14:12-14	49
14:12-16	51
14:17-18	64
14:24	96
14:58	142
15:25	65
15:29	142
15:33	66
15:34	66
15:42	50,51
15:43-45	68
15:46	68,134
16:1	38,51,69,72
16:1-2	39
16:2	34,38,42
16:4	135
16:9	34,38-9,74-5

Luke

2:12	137
2:34	87
2:34-35	87
4:16	34,139
4:18	131
4:18-19	80
5:8	90
6:1	59
6:27	7
6:45	121
7:19	80
7:22	80
7:28	131
8:15	121
10:18	113
11:29-30,32	26
11:44	19
11:51	143
13:14	33
13:16	33

Scripture Index

Scripture Index

Summary of Findings and Conclusions

Chapter 1. The Setting, The First Letter

Matthew chapter 12 provides some important context for correctly understanding the "three days and three nights in the heart of the earth."

Chapter 2. Three Days and Three Nights

Some non-Christians consider that the Bible is unbelievable if 1) Jesus was dead while Jonah was alive and 2) the timing cannot fit three days and three nights.

The comparison of Jesus to Jonah was in terms of their conditions both being, in a sense, confined or captive in their respective situations.

The Bible never uses "kardia," translated "heart," to mean in the middle or center of anything. Rather, it refers to the heart or, more accurately, the mind of man.

"Earth" is commonly used to mean the occupants of the earth. Being "in the heart of the earth," in this case, means being subject to the will or control of man.

Every reference Jesus made to the events ending with "the third day" or equivalent terms started with His betrayal which occurred on Tuesday evening.

The "three days and three nights" began Tuesday evening with Jesus' betrayal by Judas and ended with His death on Friday afternoon.

Chapter 3. His Resurrection on the Lord's Day

The Greek word "sabbaton" means the seventh-day Sabbath and there is no justification for its common translation in the phrase "first day of the week."

The resurrection occurred at or shortly after sunset on Friday evening at the beginning of the seventh-day Sabbath fulfilling the type of the Feast of First Fruits.

God's "Holy One," Jesus, did not see corruption because He was raised so soon; probably little more than three hours after His death.

He was raised before morning in fulfillment of the scripture that says: "They shall leave none of it unto the morning, nor break any bone of it … "

Chapter 4. The Timing of the Spring Feasts

Jesus and His disciples ate the Passover on Thursday evening in the early hours of Nisan 15 indicating that Passover day was actually on Thursday in that year.

References to the preparation day point to the day of the crucifixion being on Friday and thus discount the Wednesday crucifixion theory.

The Hebrew word for Sabbath "Shabbath" always refers to the seventh-day Sabbath, the seventh year or, in one case, the Day of Atonement, never to other feast days.

The "Sabbath" referred to in Leviticus 23:11, 15, 16 refers to the seventh-day Sabbath following Passover, and not to the first day of the Feast of Unleavened Bread.

The wave sheaf offering happened on the morning <u>of</u> the Sabbath not the morning <u>after</u>. Again, there is an inconsistency in translation.

Joseph's bones were "raised" on the Feast of First Fruits as the Israelites were leaving Egypt on their way to the Promised Land.

The count of 50 days from First Fruits to Pentecost always starts and ends on a seventh-day Sabbath. Both of those feasts are always on seventh-day Sabbaths.

Chapter 5. The Chronology of Events of Jesus' Last Week

Jesus entered Jerusalem as the true Lamb of God at the same time as the official ceremony of taking a lamb from Bethany to Jerusalem on Nisan 10.

Simon's feast was on Tuesday evening. Judas left from there to initiate the betrayal, beginning the three-day-and-three-night time period.

An examination of the passage about the women buying spices shows that they could have been purchased earlier. There is no need for a day between two Sabbaths.

The "next day" that the Pharisees requested the guard for the tomb was Friday evening shortly after sunset when the next day would have started.

Mary Magdalene first brought news of the resurrection not to all eleven disciples but to John's house, where he had earlier taken Mary, Jesus' mother.

Chapter 6. The Thoughts of Many Hearts Revealed

The context of Matthew 12 emphasizes that the thoughts of our hearts are revealed by the words of our mouths.

Matthew 13 includes several parables Jesus told that help to clarify what He meant by His use of the words "heart" and "earth."

Jesus Himself, as Simeon said at the dedication, was set or appointed "for a sign" so that "the thoughts of many hearts may be revealed."

The words spoken by the people involved in the crucifixion clearly revealed the thoughts of their hearts towards Jesus. And our words reveal our hearts.

Chapter 7. The Heart of the Matter

While Jesus died on Nisan 15, a day late, He also died in the wrong place, by the wrong method, and for the wrong reasons (from man's viewpoint).

Jesus words, while on the cross, showed what was in His heart. His thoughts, always for the good of others, revealed what was in the heart of God.

Jesus had to be either a liar or a lunatic or like Him – like His Father whom He claimed to represent – "He that hath seen me, hath seen the Father."

God's "wrath" is His turning from unrepentant sinners and leaving them to their choices. This was shown by His treatment of His Son who became sin for us.

The one sign only that Jesus referred to could not have been the only sign that He was the Messiah, Many such signs were given.

The sign referred to, the only sign that Jesus said would be given, was the ultimate demonstration of how far God will go to allow man to exercise his free will.

Appendices.

God allowing man to have his free will has resulted in some significant translation errors occurring in many versions of the Bible.

Something very unusual about the burial clothes John saw, convinced him that Jesus had indeed risen from the dead and that it was not a case of grave robbery.

There is no biblical basis for the idea the Jesus rested in the tomb over the Sabbath. Nor is there any need for it to support the seventh-day Sabbath.

Since the resurrection actually happened on the seventh-day Sabbath, our Friday evening, there is no support in the timing of the resurrection for Sunday sacredness.

Jesus words "destroy this Temple, and in three days I will raise it up," when the original words are examined, refer to Him being rejected not killed.

The three-day time period in Genesis 12 came before, not after, Abraham's almost-sacrifice of Isaac. The episode supports the timing presented in this book.

Additional Information

For updates, supplemental information etc. go to the website www.Jesus-resurrection.info